THE DIAMOND
THAT CUTS
THROUGH ILLUSION

THE DIAMOND
THAT CUTS
THROUGH ILLUSION

Commentaries on the Prajñaparamita Diamond Sutra

THICH NHAT HANH

Parallax Press
Berkeley, California

Parallax Press
P.O. Box 7355
Berkeley, California 94707
www.parallax.org

Parallax Press is the publishing division of Unified Buddhist Church, Inc.

The *Vajracchedika Prajñaparamita Sutra* was translated from the
Chinese by Thich Nhat Hanh, Annabel Laity, and Anh Huong
Nguyen. The commentaries were translated from the Vietnamese by
Anh Huong Nguyen.

Cover design by Gay Reineck.
Text design by Ayelet Maida.
Author photograph by Trân Van Minh.

Library of Congress Cataloging-in-Publication Data
Nhât Hanh, Thích.
    [Kim cang, guom báu chat dút phiên não. English]
    The diamond that cuts through illusion : commentaries on the
Prajñaparamita Diamond Sutra / Thich Nhat Hanh ; translated from
the Vietnamese by Anh Huong Nguyen.
        p.   cm.
Translation of: Kim cang, guom báu chat dút phiên não.
ISBN 0-938077-51-1
1. Tripitaka. Sutrapitaka. Prajñaparamita. Vajracchedika—
Commentaries. I. Nguyen, Anh Huong. II. Tripitaka.
Sutrapitaka. Prajñaparamita. Vajracchedika. English. 1992.
III. Title
BQ1997.N4413 1992
294.3'85—dc20   92-13502
                                                                CIP

10   11   12   13   14   15 / 08   07   06   05   04

Contents

PART FOUR
Mountains and Rivers Are Our Own Body

Introduction

Brothers and sisters, please read *The Diamond that Cuts through Illusion* with a serene mind, a mind free from views. Do not rush into the commentaries or you may be unduly influenced by them. Please read the sutra first. You may see things that no commentator has seen. You can read as if you were chanting, using your clear body and mind to be in touch with the words. Try to understand the sutra from your own experiences and your own suffering. It is helpful to ask, "Do these teachings of the Buddha have anything to do with my daily life?" Abstract ideas can be beautiful, but if they have nothing to do with our life, of what use are they? So please ask, "Do the words have anything to do with eating a meal, drinking tea, cutting wood, or carrying water?"

The name of this sutra is *Vajracchedika Prajñaparamita.* Vajracchedika means "the diamond that cuts through afflictions, ignorance, delusion, or illusion." In China and Vietnam, people generally call it the *Diamond Sutra,* emphasizing the word "diamond," but, in fact, the phrase "cutting through" is the most important. Therefore, please remember the sutra's full name, *The Diamond that Cuts through Illusion. Prajñaparamita* means "perfection of wisdom," "transcendent understanding," or "the understanding that brings us across the ocean of suffering to the other shore." Studying and practicing this sutra can help us cut through ignorance and wrong views and transcend them, transporting ourselves to the shore of liberation.

THE VAJRACCHEDIKA
PRAJÑAPARAMITA SUTRA

The Vajracchedika
Prajñaparamita Sutra

1

This is what I heard one time when the Buddha was staying in the monastery in Anathapindika's park in the Jeta Grove near Shravasti with a community of 1,250 bhikshus, fully ordained monks.

That day, when it was time to make the round for alms, the Buddha put on his sanghati robe and, holding his bowl, went into the city of Shravasti to seek alms food, going from house to house. When the alms round was completed, he returned to the monastery to eat the midday meal. Then he put away his sanghati robe and his bowl, washed his feet, arranged his cushion, and sat down.

2

At that time, the Venerable Subhuti stood up, bared his right shoulder, put his knee on the ground, and, folding his palms respectfully, said to the Buddha, "World-Honored One, it is rare to find someone like you. You always support and show special confidence in the bodhisattvas.

"World-Honored One, if sons and daughters of good families want to give rise to the highest, most fulfilled, awakened mind, what should they rely on and what should they do to master their thinking?"

The Buddha replied, "Well said, Subhuti! What you have said is absolutely correct. The Tathagata always supports and shows special confidence in the bodhisattvas. Please listen with all of your attention and the Tathagata will respond to your question. If daughters and sons of good families want to give rise to the highest, most fulfilled, awakened mind, they should rely on the following and master their thinking in the following way."

The Venerable Subhuti said, "Lord, we are so happy to hear your teachings."

3

The Buddha said to Subhuti, "This is how the bodhisattva mahasattvas master their thinking. 'However many species of living beings there are—whether born from eggs, from the womb, from moisture, or spontaneously; whether they have form or do not have form; whether they have perceptions or do not have perceptions; or whether it cannot be said of them that they have perceptions or that they do not have perceptions, we must lead all these beings to the ultimate nirvana so that they can be liberated. And when this innumerable, immeasurable, infinite number of beings has become liberated, we do not, in truth, think that a single being has been liberated.'

"Why is this so? If, Subhuti, a bodhisattva holds on to the idea that a self, a person, a living being, or a life span exists, that person is not an authentic bodhisattva."

4

"Moreover, Subhuti, when a bodhisattva practices generosity, he does not rely on any object—that is to say he does not rely on any form, sound, smell, taste, tactile object, or dharma—to practice generosity. That, Subhuti, is the spirit in which a bodhisattva should practice generosity, not relying on signs. Why? If a bodhisattva practices generosity without relying on signs, the happiness that results cannot be conceived of or measured. Subhuti, do you think that the space in the Eastern Quarter can be measured?"

"No, World-Honored One."

"Subhuti, can space in the Western, Southern, and Northern Quarters, above and below be measured?"

"No, World-Honored One."

"Subhuti, if a bodhisattva does not rely on any concept when practicing generosity, then the happiness that results from that virtuous act is as great as space. It cannot be measured. Subhuti, the bodhisattvas should let their minds dwell in the teachings I have just given."

5

"What do you think, Subhuti? Is it possible to grasp the Tathagata by means of bodily signs?"

"No, World-Honored One. When the Tathagata speaks of bodily signs, there are no signs being talked about."

The Buddha said to Subhuti, "In a place where there is something that can be distinguished by signs, in that place there is deception. If you can see the signless nature of signs, then you can see the Tathagata."

6

The Venerable Subhuti said to the Buddha, "In times to come, will there be people who, when they hear these teachings, have real faith and confidence in them?"

The Buddha replied, "Do not speak that way, Subhuti. Five hundred years after the Tathagata has passed away, there will still be people who enjoy the happiness that comes from observing the precepts. When such people hear these words, they will have faith and confidence that here is the truth. We should know that such people have sown seeds not only during the lifetime of one Buddha, or even two, three, four, or five Buddhas, but have, in truth, planted wholesome seeds during the lifetimes of tens of thousands of Buddhas. Anyone who, for only a second, gives rise to a pure and clear confidence upon hearing these words of the Tathagata, the Tathagata sees and knows that person, and he or she will attain immeasurable happiness because of this understanding. Why?

"Because that kind of person is not caught up in the idea of a self, a person, a living being, or a life span. They are not caught up in the idea of a dharma or the idea of a non-dharma. They are not caught up in the notion that this is a sign and that is not a sign. Why? If you are caught up in the idea of a dharma, you are also caught up in the ideas of a self, a person, a living being, and a life span. If you are caught up in the idea that there is no dharma, you are still caught up in the ideas of a self, a person, a living being, and a life span. That is why we should not get caught up in dharmas or in the idea that dharmas do not exist. This is the hidden meaning when the Tathagata says, 'Bhikshus, you should know that all of the teachings I give to you are a raft.' All teachings must be abandoned, not to mention non-teachings."

7

"What do you think, Subhuti, has the Tathagata arrived at the highest, most fulfilled, awakened mind? Does the Tathagata give any teaching?"

The Venerable Subhuti replied, "As far as I have understood the Lord Buddha's teachings, there is no independently existing object of mind called the highest, most fulfilled, awakened mind, nor is there any independently existing teaching that the Tathagata gives. Why? The teachings that the Tathagata has realized and spoken of cannot be conceived of as separate, independent existences and therefore cannot be described. The Tathagata's teaching is not self-existent nor is it non-self-existent. Why? Because the noble teachers are only distinguished from others in terms of the unconditioned."

8

"What do you think, Subhuti? If someone were to fill the 3,000 chiliocosms with the seven precious treasures as an act of generosity, would that person bring much happiness by this virtuous act?"

The Venerable Subhuti replied, "Yes, World-Honored One. It is because the very natures of virtue and happiness are not virtue and happiness that the Tathagata is able to speak about virtue and happiness."

The Buddha said, "On the other hand, if there is someone who accepts these teachings and puts them into practice, even if only a gatha of four lines, and explains them to someone else, the happiness brought about by this virtuous act far exceeds the happiness brought about by giving the seven precious treasures. Why? Because, Subhuti, all Buddhas and the dharma of the highest, most fulfilled, awakened mind of all Buddhas arise from these teachings. Subhuti, what is called Buddhadharma is everything that is not Buddhadharma."

9

"What do you think, Subhuti? Does a Stream-Enterer think, 'I have attained the fruit of stream-entry.'?"

Subhuti replied, "No, World-Honored One. Why? Stream-Enterer means to enter the stream, but in fact there is no stream to enter. One does not enter a stream that is form, nor a stream that is sound, smell, taste, touch, or object of mind. That is what we mean when we say entering a stream."

"What do you think, Subhuti? Does a Once-Returner think, 'I have attained the fruit of Once-Returning.'?"

Subhuti replied, "No, World-Honored One. Why? Once-Returner means to go and return once more, but in truth there is no going just as there is no returning. That is what we mean when we say Once-Returner."

"What do you think, Subhuti? Does a Non-Returner think like this, 'I have attained the fruit of No-Return.'?"

Subhuti replied, "No, World-Honored One. Why? No-Return means not to return to this world, but in fact there cannot be any Non-Returning. That is what we mean when we say Non-Returner."

"What do you think, Subhuti? Does an Arhat think like this, 'I have attained the fruit of Arhatship.'?"

Subhuti replied, "No, World-Honored One. Why? There is no separately existing thing that can be called Arhat. If an Arhat gives rise to the thought that he has attained the fruit of Arhatship, then he is still caught up in the idea of a self, a person, a living being, and a life span. World-Honored One, you have often said that I have attained the concentration of peaceful abiding and that in the community, I am the Arhat who has most transformed need and desire. World-Honored

One, if I were to think that I had attained the fruit of Arhatship, you certainly would not have said that I love to dwell in the concentration of peaceful abiding."

10

The Buddha asked Subhuti, "In ancient times when the Tathagata practiced under Buddha Dipankara, did he attain anything?"

Subhuti answered, "No, World-Honored One. In ancient times when the Tathagata was practicing under Buddha Dipankara, he did not attain anything."

"What do you think, Subhuti? Does a bodhisattva create a serene and beautiful Buddha field?"

"No, World-Honored One. Why? To create a serene and beautiful Buddha field is not in fact creating a serene and beautiful Buddha field. That is why it is called creating a serene and beautiful Buddha field."

The Buddha said, "So, Subhuti, all the bodhisattva mahasattvas should give rise to a pure and clear intention in this spirit. When they give rise to this intention, they should not rely on forms, sounds, smells, tastes, tactile objects, or objects of mind. They should give rise to an intention with their minds not dwelling anywhere."

"Subhuti, if there were someone with a body as big as Mount Sumeru, would you say that his was a large body?"

Subhuti answered, "Yes, World-Honored One, very large. Why? What the Tathagata says is not a large body, that is known as a large body."

11

"Subhuti, if there were as many Ganges Rivers as the number of grains of sand in the Ganges, would you say that the number of grains of sand in all those Ganges Rivers is very many?"

Subhuti answered, "Very many indeed, World-Honored One. If the number of Ganges Rivers were huge, how much more so the number of grains of sand in all those Ganges Rivers."

"Subhuti, now I want to ask you this: if a daughter or son of good family were to fill the 3,000 chiliocosms with as many precious jewels as the number of grains of sand in all the Ganges Rivers as an act of generosity, would that person bring much happiness by her virtuous act?"

Subhuti replied, "Very much, World-Honored One."

The Buddha said to Subhuti, "If a daughter or son of a good family knows how to accept, practice, and explain this sutra to others, even if it is a gatha of four lines, the happiness that results from this virtuous act would be far greater."

12

"Furthermore, Subhuti, any plot of land on which this sutra is proclaimed, even if only one gatha of four lines, will be a land where gods, men, and asuras will come to make offerings just as they make offerings to a stupa of the Buddha. If the plot of land is regarded as that sacred, how much more so the person who practices and recites this sutra. Subhuti, you should know that that person attains something rare and profound. Wherever this sutra is kept is a sacred site enshrining the presence of the Buddha or one of the Buddha's great disciples."

13

After that, Subhuti asked the Buddha, "What should this sutra be called and how should we act regarding its teachings?"

The Buddha replied, "This sutra should be called *The Diamond that Cuts through Illusion* because it has the capacity to cut through all illusions and afflictions and bring us to the shore of liberation. Please use this title and practice according to its deepest meaning. Why? What the Tathagata has called the highest, transcendent understanding is not, in fact, the highest, transcendent understanding. That is why it is truly the highest, transcendent understanding."

The Buddha asked, "What do you think, Subhuti? Is there any dharma that the Tathagata teaches?"

Subhuti replied, "The Tathagata has nothing to teach, World-Honored One."

"What do you think, Subhuti? Are there many particles of dust in the 3,000 chiliocosms?"

"Very many, World-Honored One."

"Subhuti, the Tathagata says that these particles of dust are not particles of dust. That is why they are truly particles of dust. And what the Tathagata calls chiliocosms are not in fact chiliocosms. That is why they are called chiliocosms."

"What do you think, Subhuti? Can the Tathagata be recognized by the possession of the thirty-two marks?"

The Venerable Subhuti replied, "No, World-Honored One. Why? Because what the Tathagata calls the thirty-two marks are not essentially marks and that is why the Tathagata calls them the thirty-two marks."

"Subhuti, if as many times as there are grains of sand in the Ganges a son or daughter of a good family gives up his or her life as an act of generosity and if another daughter or son of a good family knows how to accept, practice, and explain this sutra to others, even if only a gatha of four lines, the happiness resulting from explaining this sutra is far greater."

14

When he had heard this much and penetrated deeply into its significance, the Venerable Subhuti was moved to tears. He said, "World-Honored One, you are truly rare in this world. Since the day I attained the eyes of understanding, thanks to the guidance of the Buddha, I have never before heard teachings so deep and wonderful as these. World-Honored One, if someone hears this sutra, has pure and clear confidence in it, and arrives at insight into the truth, that person will realize the rarest kind of virtue. World-Honored One, that insight into the truth is essentially not insight. That is what the Tathagata calls insight into the truth.

"World-Honored One, today it is not difficult for me to hear this wonderful sutra, have confidence in it, understand it, accept it, and put it into practice. But in the future, in 500 years, if there is someone who can hear this sutra, have confidence in it, understand it, accept it, and put it into practice, then certainly the existence of someone like that will be great and rare. Why? That person will not be dominated by the idea of a self, a person, a living being, or a life span. Why? The idea of a self is not an idea, and the ideas of a person, a living being, and a life span are not ideas either. Why? Buddhas are called Buddhas because they are free of ideas."

"The Buddha said to Subhuti, "That is quite right. If someone hears this sutra and is not terrified or afraid, he or she is rare. Why? Subhuti, what the Tathagata calls *parama-paramita*, the highest transcendence, is not essentially the highest transcendence, and that is why it is called the highest transcendence.

"Subhuti, the Tathagata has said that what is called transcendent endurance is not transcendent endurance. That is why it is called transcendent endurance. Why? Subhuti, thousands of lifetimes ago when my body was cut into pieces by King Kalinga, I was not caught in the idea of a self, a person, a living being, or a life span. If, at that time, I had been caught up in any of those ideas, I would have felt anger and ill-will against the king.

"I also remember in ancient times, for 500 lifetimes, I practiced transcendent endurance by not being caught up in the idea of a self, a person, a living being, or a life span. So, Subhuti, when a bodhisattva gives rise to the unequalled mind of awakening, he has to give up all ideas. He cannot rely on forms when he gives rise to that mind, nor on sounds, smells, tastes, tactile objects, or objects of mind. He can only give rise to that mind that is not caught up in anything.

"The Tathagata has said that all notions are not notions and that all living beings are not living beings. Subhuti, the Tathagata is one who speaks of things as they are, speaks what is true, and speaks in accord with reality. He does not speak deceptively or to please people. Subhuti, if we say that the Tathagata has realized a teaching, that teaching is neither graspable nor deceptive.

"Subhuti, a bodhisattva who still depends on notions to practice generosity is like someone walking in the dark. He will not see anything. But when a bodhisattva does not depend on notions to practice generosity, he is like someone with good eyesight walking under the bright light of the sun. He can see all shapes and colors.

"Subhuti, if in the future there is any daughter or son of good family who has the capacity to accept, read, and put into practice this sutra, the Tathagata will see that person with his eyes of understanding. The Tathagata will know that person, and that person will realize the measureless, limitless fruit of her or his virtuous act."

15

"Subhuti, if on the one hand, a daughter or son of a good family gives up her or his life in the morning as many times as there are grains of sand in the Ganges as an act of generosity, and gives as many again in the afternoon and as many again in the evening, and continues doing so for countless ages; and if, on the other hand, another person listens to this sutra with complete confidence and without contention, that person's happiness will be far greater. But the happiness of one who writes this sutra down, receives, recites, and explains it to others cannot be compared.

"In summary, Subhuti, this sutra brings about boundless virtue and happiness that cannot be conceived or measured. If there is someone capable of receiving, practicing, reciting, and sharing this sutra with others, the Tathagata will see and know that person, and he or she will have inconceivable, indescribable, and incomparable virtue. Such a person will be able to shoulder the highest, most fulfilled, awakened career of the Tathagata. Why? Subhuti, if one is content with the small teachings, if he or she is still caught up in the idea of a self, a person, a living being, or a life span, he or she will not be able to listen, receive, recite, and explain this sutra to others. Subhuti, any place this sutra is found is a place where gods, men, and asuras will come to make offerings. Such a place is a shrine and should be venerated with formal ceremonies, circumambulations, and offerings of flowers and incense."

16

"Furthermore, Subhuti, if a son or daughter of good family, while reciting and practicing this sutra, is disdained or slandered, his or her misdeeds committed in past lives, including those that could bring about an evil destiny, will be eradicated, and he or she will attain the fruit of the most fulfilled, awakened mind. Subhuti, in ancient times before I met Buddha Dipankara, I had made offerings to and had been attendant of all 84,000 multi-millions of buddhas. If someone is able to receive, recite, study, and practice this sutra in the last epoch, the happiness brought about by this virtuous act is hundreds of thousands times greater than that which I brought about in ancient times. In fact, such happiness cannot be conceived or compared with anything, even mathematically. Such happiness is immeasurable.

"Subhuti, the happiness resulting from the virtuous act of a son or daughter of good family who receives, recites, studies, and practices this sutra in the last epoch will be so great that if I were to explain it now in detail, some people would become suspicious and disbelieving, and their minds might become disoriented. Subhuti, you should know that the meaning of this sutra is beyond conception and discussion. Likewise, the fruit resulting from receiving and practicing this sutra is beyond conception and discussion."

17

At that time, the Venerable Subhuti said to the Buddha, "World-Honored One, may I ask you again that if daughters or sons of good family want to give rise to the highest, most fulfilled, awakened mind, what should they rely on and what should they do to master their thinking?"

The Buddha replied, "Subhuti, a good son or daughter who wants to give rise to the highest, most fulfilled, awakened mind should do it in this way: 'We must lead all beings to the shore of awakening, but, after these beings have become liberated, we do not, in truth, think that a single being has been liberated.' Why is this so? Subhuti, if a bodhisattva is still caught up in the idea of a self, a person, a living being or a life span, that person is not an authentic bodhisattva. Why is that?

"Subhuti, in fact, there is no independently existing object of mind called the highest, most fulfilled, awakened mind. What do you think, Subhuti? In ancient times, when the Tathagata was living with Buddha Dipankara, did he attain anything called the highest, most fulfilled, awakened mind?"

"No, World-Honored One. According to what I understand from the teachings of the Buddha, there is no attaining of anything called the highest, most fulfilled, awakened mind."

The Buddha said, "Right you are, Subhuti. In fact, there does not exist the so-called highest, most fulfilled, awakened mind that the Tathagata attains. Because if there had been any such thing, Buddha Dipankara would not have predicted of me, 'In the future, you will come to be a Buddha called Shakyamuni.' This prediction was made because there is, in fact, nothing that can be attained that is called the highest, most fulfilled, awakened mind. Why? Tathagata means the suchness of all things (dharmas). Someone would be mistaken to say that the Tathagata has attained the highest, most fulfilled, awakened mind since there is not any highest, most fulfilled, awakened mind to be attained. Subhuti, the highest, most fulfilled, awakened mind that the Tathagata has attained is neither graspable nor elusive. This is why the Tathagata has said, 'All dharmas are Buddhadharma.' What are called all dharmas are, in fact, not all dharmas. That is why they are called all dharmas.

"Subhuti, a comparison can be made with the idea of a great human body."

Subhuti said, "What the Tathagata calls a great human body is, in fact, not a great human body."

"Subhuti, it is the same concerning bodhisattvas. If a bodhisattva thinks that she has to liberate all living beings, then she is not yet a bodhisattva. Why? Subhuti, there is no independently existing object of mind called bodhisattva. Therefore, the Buddha has said that all dharmas are without a self, a person, a living being, or a life span. Subhuti, if a bodhisattva thinks, 'I have to create a serene and beautiful Buddha field,' that person is not yet a bodhisattva. Why? What the Tathagata calls a serene and beautiful Buddha field is not in fact a serene and beautiful Buddha field. And that is why it is called a serene and beautiful Buddha field. Subhuti, any bodhisattva who thoroughly understands the principle of non-self and non-dharma is called by the Tathagata an authentic bodhisattva."

18

"Subhuti, what do you think? Does the Tathagata have the human eye?"

Subhuti replied, "Yes, World-Honored One, the Tathagata does have the human eye."

The Buddha asked, "Subhuti, what do you think? Does the Tathagata have the divine eye?"

Subhuti said, "Yes, World-Honored One, the Tathagata does have the divine eye."

"Subhuti, what do you think? Does the Tathagata have the eye of insight?"

Subhuti replied, "Yes, World-Honored One, the Tathagata does have the eye of insight."

"Subhuti, what do you think? Does the Tathagata have the eye of transcendent wisdom?"

"Yes, World-Honored One, the Tathagata does have the eye of transcendent wisdom."

The Buddha asked, "Does the Tathagata have the Buddha eye?"

"Yes, World-Honored One, the Tathagata does have the Buddha eye."

"Subhuti, what do you think? Does the Buddha see the sand in the Ganges as sand?"

Subhuti said, "World-Honored One, the Tathagata also calls it sand."

"Subhuti, if there were as many Ganges Rivers as the number of grains of sand of the Ganges and there was a Buddha land for each grain of sand in all those Ganges Rivers, would those Buddha lands be many?"

"Yes, World-Honored One, very many."

The Buddha said, "Subhuti, however many living beings there are in all these Buddha lands, though they each have a different mentality, the Tathagata understands them all. Why is that? Subhuti, what the Tathagata calls different mentalities are not in fact different mentalities. That is why they are called different mentalities."

"Why? Subhuti, the past mind cannot be grasped, neither can the present mind or the future mind."

19

"What do you think, Subhuti? If someone were to fill the 3,000 chiliocosms with precious treasures as an act of generosity, would that person bring great happiness by his virtuous act?"

"Yes, very much, World-Honored One."

"Subhuti, if such happiness were conceived as an entity separate from everything else, the Tathagata would not have said it to be great, but because it is ungraspable, the Tathagata has said that the virtuous act of that person brought about great happiness."

20

"Subhuti, what do you think? Can the Tathagata be perceived by his perfectly formed body?"

"No, World-Honored One. What the Tathagata calls a perfectly formed body is not in fact a perfectly formed body. That is why it is called a perfectly formed body."

"What do you think, Subhuti? Can the Tathagata be perceived by his perfectly formed physiognomy?"

"No, World-Honored One. It is impossible to perceive the Tathagata by any perfectly formed physiognomy. Why?

Because what the Tathagata calls perfectly formed physiognomy is not in fact perfectly formed physiognomy. That is why it is called perfectly formed physiognomy."

21

"Subhuti, do not say that the Tathagata conceives the idea 'I will give a teaching.' Do not think that way. Why? If anyone says that the Tathagata has something to teach, that person slanders the Buddha because he does not understand what I say. Subhuti, giving a Dharma talk in fact means that no talk is given. This is truly a Dharma talk."

Then, Insight-Life Subhuti said to the Buddha, "World-Honored One, in the future, will there be living beings who will feel complete confidence when they hear these words?"

The Buddha said, "Subhuti, those living beings are neither living beings nor non-living beings. Why is that? Subhuti, what the Tathagata calls non-living beings are truly living beings."

22

Subhuti asked the Buddha, "World-Honored One, is the highest, most fulfilled, awakened mind that the Buddha attained the unattainable?"

The Buddha said, "That is right, Subhuti. Regarding the highest, most fulfilled, awakened mind, I have not attained anything. That is why it is called the highest, most fulfilled, awakened mind."

23

"Furthermore, Subhuti, that mind is everywhere equally. Because it is neither high nor low, it is called the highest, most fulfilled, awakened mind. The fruit of the highest, most fulfilled, awakened mind is realized through the practice of all wholesome actions in the spirit of non-self, non-person, non-living being, and non-life span. Subhuti, what are called wholesome actions are in fact not wholesome actions. That is why they are called wholesome actions."

24

"Subhuti, if someone were to fill the 3,000 chiliocosms with piles of the seven precious treasures as high as Mount Sumeru as an act of generosity, the happiness resulting from this is much less than that of another person who knows how to accept, practice, and explain the *Vajracchedika Prajñaparamita Sutra* to others. The happiness resulting from the virtue of a person who practices this sutra, even if it is only a gatha of four lines, cannot be described by using examples or mathematics."

25

"Subhuti, do not say that the Tathagata has the idea, 'I will bring living beings to the shore of liberation.' Do not think that way, Subhuti. Why? In truth there is not one single being for the Tathagata to bring to the other shore. If the Tathagata were to think there was, he would be caught in the idea of a self, a person, a living being, or a life span. Subhuti, what the Tathagata calls a self essentially has no self in the way that ordinary persons think there is a self. Subhuti, the

Tathagata does not regard anyone as an ordinary person. That is why he can call them ordinary persons."

26

"What do you think, Subhuti? Can someone meditate on the Tathagata by means of the thirty-two marks?"

Subhuti said, "Yes, World-Honored One. We should use the thirty-two marks to meditate on the Tathagata."

The Buddha said, "If you say that you can use the thirty-two marks to see the Tathagata, then the Cakravartin is also a Tathagata?"

Subhuti said, "World-Honored One, I understand your teaching. One should not use the thirty-two marks to meditate on the Tathagata."

Then the World-Honored One spoke this verse:

"Someone who looks for me in form
or seeks me in sound
is on a mistaken path
and cannot see the Tathagata."

27

"Subhuti, if you think that the Tathagata realizes the highest, most fulfilled, awakened mind and does not need to have all the marks, you are wrong. Subhuti, do not think in that way. Do not think that when one gives rise to the highest, most fulfilled, awakened mind, one needs to see all objects of mind as nonexistent, cut off from life. Please do not think in that way. One who gives rise to the highest, most fulfilled, awakened mind does not contend that all objects of mind are nonexistent and cut off from life."

28

"Subhuti, if a bodhisattva were to fill the 3,000 chiliocosms with the seven precious treasures as many as the number of sand grains in the Ganges as an act of generosity, the happiness brought about by his or her virtue is less than that brought about by someone who has understood and wholeheartedly accepted the truth that all dharmas are of selfless nature and is able to live and bear fully this truth. Why is that, Subhuti? Because a bodhisattva does not need to build up virtue and happiness."

Subhuti asked the Buddha, "What do you mean, World-Honored One, when you say that a bodhisattva does not need to build up virtue and happiness?"

"Subhuti, a bodhisattva gives rise to virtue and happiness but is not caught in the idea of virtue and happiness. That is why the Tathagata has said that a bodhisattva does not need to build up virtue and happiness."

29

"Subhuti, if someone says that the World-Honored One comes, goes, sits, and lies down, that person has not understood what I have said. Why? The meaning of Tathagata is 'does not come from anywhere and does not go anywhere.' That is why he is called a Tathagata."

30

"Subhuti, if a daughter or son of a good family were to grind the 3,000 chiliocosms to particles of dust, do you think there would be many particles?"

Subhuti replied, "World-Honored One, there would be many indeed. Why? If particles of dust had a real self-existence, the Buddha would not have called them particles of dust. What the Buddha calls particles of dust are not, in essence, particles of dust. That is why they can be called particles of dust. World-Honored One, what the Tathagata calls the 3,000 chiliocosms are not chiliocosms. That is why they are called chiliocosms. Why? If chiliocosms are real, they are a compound of particles under the conditions of being assembled into an object. That which the Tathagata calls a compound is not essentially a compound. That is why it is called a compound."

"Subhuti, what is called a compound is just a conventional way of speaking. It has no real basis. Only ordinary people are caught up in conventional terms."

31

"Subhuti, if anyone says that the Buddha has spoken of a self view, a person view, a living-being view, or a life span view, has that person understood my meaning?"

"No, World-Honored One. Such a person has not understood the Tathagata. Why? What the Tathagata calls a self view, a person view, a living-being view, or a life span view are not in essence a self view, a person view, a living-being view, or a life span view. That is why they are called a self view, a person view, a living-being view, or a life span view."

"Subhuti, someone who gives rise to the highest, most fulfilled, awakened mind should know that this is true of all dharmas, should see that all dharmas are like this, should have confidence in the understanding of all dharmas without any conceptions about dharmas. Subhuti, what is called a conception of dharmas, the Tathagata has said, is not a conception of dharmas. That is why it is called a conception of dharmas."

32

"Subhuti, if someone were to offer an immeasurable quantity of the seven treasures to fill the worlds as infinite as space as an act of generosity, the happiness resulting from that virtuous act would not equal the happiness resulting from a son or daughter of a good family who gives rise to the awakened mind and reads, recites, accepts, and puts into practice this sutra, and explains it to others, even if only a gatha of four lines. In what spirit is this explanation given? Without being caught up in signs, just according to things as they are, without agitation. Why is this?

> "All composed things are like a dream,
> a phantom, a drop of dew, a flash of lightning.
> That is how to meditate on them,
> that is how to observe them."

After they heard the Lord Buddha deliver this sutra, the Venerable Subhuti, the bhikshus and bhikshunis, laymen and laywomen, and gods and asuras, filled with joy and confidence, undertook to put these teachings into practice.

THE COMMENTARIES

PART ONE

The Dialectics of Prajñaparamita

1
THE SETTING

This is what I heard one time when the Buddha was staying in the monastery in Anathapindika's park in the Jeta Grove near Shravasti with a community of 1,250 bhikshus, fully ordained monks.

The first sentence of the sutra tells us that the Buddha gave this discourse to 1,250 monks. It does not say that innumerable bodhisattvas from different worlds gathered to hear the Buddha. This detail demonstrates that *The Diamond that Cuts through Illusion* is among the earliest of the prajñaparamita sutras. Although the Buddha mentions bodhisattvas in this sutra, the audience at the time was almost entirely shravakas, his noble disciples.

That day, when it was time to make the round for alms, the Buddha put on his sanghati robe and, holding his bowl, went into the city of Shravasti to seek alms food, going from house to house. When the alms round was completed, he returned to the monastery to eat the midday meal. Then he put away his sanghati robe and his bowl, washed his feet, arranged his cushion, and sat down.

This activity was repeated day after day by the monks in the Anathapindika Monastery, as well as in all of the Buddha's monasteries. The Buddha taught his monks and nuns not to distinguish between rich and poor homes when going for alms food, just to go from one dwelling to the next. Seeking alms food is a way to cultivate non-discriminating mind and also to be in touch with different classes of people to guide them in the practices taught by the Buddha. Even if a monk knew that the people in a particular house would be unkind and not offer him food, he still had to go there and stand still for a few minutes before moving along to the next house.

2
SUBHUTI'S QUESTION

At that time, the Venerable Subhuti stood up, bared his right shoulder, put his knee on the ground, and, folding his palms respectfully, said to the Buddha, "World-Honored One, it is rare to find someone like you. You always support and show special confidence in the bodhisattvas."

The student, Subhuti, begins this discourse by praising his teacher and then asking an important question. He says that it is rare to find someone like the Buddha, who always gives full support and shows special confidence in the bodhisattvas.

Bodhisattvas are compassionate people whose intention is to relieve their own suffering and the suffering of their fellow beings. Just like a young Vietnamese student who always makes the effort to succeed so that he can take care of his parents and siblings who are still in Vietnam, the bodhisattvas practice not only for themselves but for their families, communities, and the entire society. One Vietnamese college student in Bordeaux has a sign on his desk that says, "I clench my teeth in order to succeed." There are so many temptations and distractions, and he knows that if he is carried away by any of them, he will ruin his parents' hopes and expectations. Because of his firm determination, he is like a bodhisattva and those on the path of practice. When we meet someone like this, compassion wells up in us. We want to help and support him. It is a waste of energy to support those who live only for themselves and forget about others. This is why the Buddha gives special attention and offers care and support to those with the mind and heart of a bodhisattva. It is not because he is discriminating, but because he knows that it is a good investment.

I always invest in young people. It is not that I discriminate against older people, but, in my country, after many long and painful wars, the minds of the older people are wounded and confused, and it is safer to invest in the young people. Our people are less beautiful than they were in the past. There is so much suspicion, hatred, and misunderstanding. Weeds and thorns have grown everywhere in the soil of their minds. If we sow healthy seeds in such depleted soil, perhaps a few will sprout, but if we sow the same seeds in the fertile minds of young people whose wounds of war are relatively few, most of them are likely to sprout. This is a good investment. Of course, we should also support the older people, but since our time and energy are limited, sowing seeds in the most fertile land has to be our priority.

In the *Pali Canon*, a layman asks the Buddha why he gives more care and attention to monks and nuns than to laypersons. The Buddha answers that he does so because monks and nuns spend all of their time and energy practicing the way. Their spiritual land is richer, so the Buddha invests more of his time in cultivating it. Subhuti, an elder monk with the title *Mahathera*, "Great Elder," notices that the Buddha has been paying special attention to the bodhisattvas, and he asks him about it. The Buddha confirms that he does give special support to those whose determination is to help all living beings, and he also gives them a lot of responsibility.

"World-Honored One, if sons and daughters of good families want to give rise to the highest, most fulfilled, awakened mind, what should they rely on and what should they do to master their thinking?"

The Buddha replied, "Well said, Subhuti! What you have said is absolutely correct. The Tathagata always supports and shows special confidence in the bodhisattvas. Please listen with all of your attention and the Tathagata will respond to your question. If daughters and sons of good families want to give rise to the highest, most fulfilled, awakened mind, they should rely on the following and master their thinking in the following way."

The Venerable Subhuti said, "Lord, we are so happy to hear your teachings."

"Bodhi" means awake. "Sattva" means living being. A bodhisattva is an awakened being who helps other beings wake up. Humans are only one kind of living being. Other living beings also have the potential to awaken. When we enter the path of awakening, our mind is determined to practice. To give rise to a bodhisattva mind, that is, to the deepest understanding and the greatest ability to help others, where should our mind take refuge and how can we master our thinking? The *Diamond Sutra* is a response to this question.

3
THE FIRST FLASH OF LIGHTNING

The Buddha said to Subhuti, "This is how the bodhisattva mahasattvas master their thinking. 'However many species of living beings there are—whether born from eggs, from the womb, from moisture, or spontaneously; whether they have form or do not have form; whether they have perceptions or do not have perceptions; or whether it cannot be said of them that they have perceptions or that they do not have perceptions, we must lead all these beings to the ultimate nirvana so that they can be liberated.'"

The word *maha* means "great," so *mahasattva* means "a great being." Liberation here means arriving at *nirvana*, "extinction," a joyful, peaceful state in which all causes of afflictions have been uprooted and we are totally free. The mahasattvas take the great vow to relieve the suffering of all living beings, to bring all to absolute nirvana where they can realize ultimate peace and joy. Absolute nirvana is also called "nirvana without residue of affliction," as compared to nirvana with some residue of afflictions. Some commentators explain that nirvana with some residue of afflictions is a state in which the body of the five aggregates (form, feelings, perceptions, mental formations, and consciousness) still exists. They regard the body as a residue of the afflictions of our previous lives. After we die, they say, the body of the five aggregates disintegrates completely, and we enter "nirvana without residue of affliction," leaving no trace behind.

I do not fully agree. It is true that once we put an end to the causes of suffering and transform them, we will not bring about new consequences of suffering in the future. But what has existed for a long time, even after it is cut off, still has momentum and will continue for a while before stopping completely. When an electric fan is switched off, although the current has been cut, the blades keep moving for a while longer. Even after the cause has been cut off, the consequence of this past cause continues for a while. The residue of afflictions is the same. What comes to a stop is the creation of new causes of suffering, not the body of the five aggregates. One day, Devadatta threw a rock at the Buddha, and his foot was wounded. The Buddha was no longer creating new karma, but he experienced this karmic consequence as the result of a past action that had some energy left over before it could stop. This does not mean that the Buddha had not realized complete extinction after he passed away.

The Mahayana sutras say that bodhisattvas ride on the waves of birth and death. Riding on the waves of birth and death means that although birth and death are there, they are not drowned by them. While traveling in the ocean of birth and death, the bodhisattvas are in perfect nirvana, that is, nirvana without any residue of afflictions—not in the imperfect nirvana that has some residue of afflictions. Although their bodies are there and they are riding on birth and death, they do not suffer. Therefore the residues of afflictions in the imperfect nirvana are not the five aggregates themselves, but rather the afflictions that remain as the karmic consequence of past actions.

"However many species of living beings there are—whether born from eggs, from the womb, from moisture, or spontaneously; whether they have form or do not have form; whether they have perceptions or do not have perceptions; or whether it cannot be said of them that they have perceptions or that they do not have perceptions, we must lead all these beings to the ultimate nirvana so that they can be liberated."

This sentence exemplifies the bodhisattva's Great Vow. It is the prerequisite of becoming a bodhisattva, an awakened person, a person for whom the work for enlightenment is his or her life work, a person who is called a great being, a person to whom the Buddha gives special support and attention. This vow is not only the basic condition of being a bodhisattva, it is also the primary condition. It is the foundation of the highest, most fulfilling wish of a bodhisattva.

When we read this passage, we must look at ourselves and ask, "Is this vow at all related to my life and the life of my community? Are we practicing for ourselves or for others? Do we only want to uproot our own afflictions, or is our determination to study and practice to bring happiness to other living beings?" If we look at ourselves, we will see if we are among the bodhisattvas the Buddha is addressing, supporting, and investing in. If we study and practice with a heart like this, we won't have to wait several years for others to notice. They will see it right away by the way we treat the cat, the caterpillar, or the snail. When we wash the dishes, do we put the leftover food aside to feed the birds? These kinds of small acts show our love for all living beings. The great heart of a bodhisattva mahasattva can be seen throughout his or her daily life. While studying the bodhisattva's actions in the Mahayana sutras, we should also practice looking at ourselves—the way we drink tea, eat our food, wash the dishes, or tend our garden. If we observe ourselves in this way, we will see whether we have the understanding of a bodhisattva, and our friends will also know.

The living beings mentioned in this sutra are not only remote strangers. They are the brothers and sisters with whom we study and practice the Dharma. They too have joy and pain, and we must see them and be open to them. If we are only an independent island, living in a community but not seeing or smiling with the community, we are not practicing as a bodhisattva. Besides just our Dharma brothers and sisters, there are also other species of animals, as well as the plants in the garden and the stars in the sky. This sutra is addressing all of them, and explaining how all are related to our daily life and practice. If we are mindful, we will see.

"And when this innumerable, immeasurable, infinite number of beings has become liberated, we do not, in truth, think that a single being has been liberated."

This is the first flash of lightning. The Buddha goes directly to the heart of the prajñaparamita, presenting the principle of formlessness. He tells us that a true practitioner helps all living beings in a natural and spontaneous way, without distinguishing between the one who is helping and the one who is being helped. When our left hand is injured, our right hand takes care of it right away. It doesn't stop to say, "I am taking care of you. You are benefiting from my compassion." The right hand knows very well that the left hand is also the right hand. There is no distinction between them. This is the principle of interbeing—co-existence, or mutual interdependence. "This is because that is." With this understanding—the right hand helping the left hand in a formless way—there is no need to distinguish between the right hand and the left hand.

For a bodhisattva, the work of helping is natural, like breathing. When her brother suffers, she offers care and support. She does not think that she has to help him in order to practice the Dharma or because her teacher says she should. It isn't necessary to have an idea of helping. We feel the need to do it, and we do it. This is easy to understand. If we act in this spirit of formlessness, we will not say, later on, "When my brother was sick, I took care of him every day. I made him soup and did many other things for him, and now he is not at all grateful." If we speak like that, our actions were done in the spirit of form. That is not what is called a good deed according to the teaching of prajñaparamita. Formlessness is something concrete that we can put into practice here and now.

If someone in your community is lazy and does not work hard when everyone else does, you may think, "She is awful. She stays in her room and listens to music while I have to work hard." The more you think about her, the more uncomfortable you become. In that state, your work does not bring happiness to you or anyone else. You should be able to enjoy what you are doing. Why should the absence of one person affect your work so? If, when you are working, you do not distinguish between the person who is doing the work and the one who is not, that is truly the spirit of form-lessness. We can apply the practice of prajñaparamita into every aspect of our lives. We can wash the dishes or clean the bathroom in exactly the way our right hand puts a band-aid on our left hand, without discrimination.

When the Buddha says, "When innumerable, immeasur-able, infinite beings become liberated, we do not think that a single being has been liberated," these are not empty words. The Buddha is encouraging us to support and love *all* living beings. It would be wonderful if those who study Bud-dhism understood this one sentence. The teaching here is so complete and profound.

"Why is this so? If, Subhuti, a bodhisattva holds on to the idea that a self, a person, a living being, or a life span exists, that person is not an authentic bodhisattva."

Our right hand is an authentic bodhisattva, because it does not discriminate between itself and our left hand. There is just "taking care."

The words "self," "person," "living being," and "life span" are important for us to understand. "Self" refers to a perma-nent, changeless identity, but since, according to Buddhism, nothing is permanent and what we normally call a self is made entirely of non-self elements, there is really no such entity as a self. Our concept of self arises when we have con-cepts about things that are not-self. Using the sword of conceptualization to cut reality into pieces, we call one part "I" and the rest "not I."

The concept of "person," like the concept of self, is made only of non-person elements—sun, clouds, wheat, space, and so on. Thanks to these elements, there is something we call a person. But erecting a barrier between the idea of person and the idea of non-person is erroneous. If we say, for example, that the cosmos has given birth to humankind and that other animals, plants, the moon, the stars, and so forth, exist to serve us, we are caught up in the idea of person. These kinds of concepts are used to separate self from non-self and person from non-person, and they are erroneous.

We put a lot of energy into advancing technology in order to serve our lives better, and we exploit the non-human elements, such as the forests, rivers, and oceans, in order to do so. But as we pollute and destroy nature, we pollute and destroy ourselves as well. The results of discriminating between human and non-human are global warming, pollution, and the emergence of many strange diseases. In order to protect ourselves, we must protect the non-human elements. This fundamental understanding is needed if we want to protect our planet and ourselves.

The concept of "living being," *sattva* in Sanskrit, arises the moment we separate living from non-living beings. The poet Lamartine once asked, "Inanimate objects, do you have a soul?" to challenge our popular understanding. But what we call non-living makes what we call living beings possible. If we destroy the non-living, we also destroy the living. In Buddhist monasteries, during the Ceremony of Beginning Anew, each monk and nun recites, "I vow to practice wholeheartedly so that all beings, living and non-living, will be liberated." In many ceremonies, we bow deeply to show our gratitude to our parents, teachers, friends, and numerous beings in the animal, vegetal, and mineral worlds. Doing this helps us realize that there is no separation between the living and the so-called non-living. Vietnamese composer Trinh Cong Con wrote, "How do we know the stones are not suffering? Tomorrow the pebbles will need one another." When we really understand love, our love will include all beings, living and so-called non-living.

We usually think of "life span" as the length of our life, beginning the moment we are born and ending when we die. We believe that we are alive during that period, not before or after. And while we are alive, we think that everything in us is life, not death. Once again, the sword of conceptualization is cutting reality into pieces, separating one side, life, from the other side, death. But to think that we begin our life at the moment we are born and end it the moment we die is an erroneous view, called the "view of life span." According to prajñaparamita, life and death are one. We are born and die during every second of our life. During one so-called life span, there are millions of births and millions of deaths. Cells in our body cease to be every day—brain cells, skin cells, blood cells, and many, many others. Our planet is also a body, and we are each a cell in that body. Must we cry and organize a funeral every time one cell of our body or one cell of the Earth's body dies? Death is necessary for life to be. In the *Samyutta Nikaya,* the Buddha says, "When causes and conditions are sufficient, eyes are present. When causes and conditions are not sufficient, eyes are absent. The same is true of body and consciousness." We love life and grasp it tightly. We dread death and want to hide from it. Doing this brings us much worry and anxiety and is caused entirely by our view of life span.

The Sanskrit word for "perception" is *samjña.* According to the *Vijñanavadin* school of Buddhist psychology, perception has two components—a subject and an object of cognition. Walking in the woods at night, if we see a snake, we will probably feel very frightened. But if we shine our flashlight on it and see that it is just a rope, we will feel a great relief. Seeing the snake was an erroneous perception, and the Buddha teaches us that four erroneous perceptions are at the root of our suffering—perception of (1) a self, (2) a person, (3) a living being, and (4) a life span. A bodhisattva is someone who is free from all of these wrong perceptions.

We all enjoy leaving the city and going to the countryside. The trees are so beautiful; the air is so fresh. For me, this is one of the great pleasures of life. In the countryside, I like to walk slowly in the woods, look deeply at the trees and flowers, and, when I have to pee, I can do so right in the open air. The fresh air is so much more pleasant than any bathroom in the city, especially some very smelly public restrooms. But I have to confess that for years I was uneasy about peeing in the woods. The moment I approached a tree, I felt so much respect for its beauty and grandeur that I couldn't bring myself to pee right in front of it. It seemed impolite, even disrespectful. So I would walk somewhere else, but there was always another tree or bush, and I felt equally disrespectful there.

We usually think of our bathroom at home, made of wood, tile, or cement, as inanimate and we have no problem peeing there. But after I studied the *Diamond Sutra* and I saw that wood, tile, and cement are also marvelous and animate, I began to even feel uncomfortable using my own bathroom. Then I had a realization. I realized that peeing is also a marvelous and wondrous reality, our gift to the universe. We only have to pee mindfully, with great respect for ourselves and whatever surroundings we are in. So now I can pee in nature, fully respectful of the trees, the bushes, and myself. Through studying the *Diamond Sutra*, I solved this dilemma, and I enjoy being in the countryside now more than ever.

4
THE GREATEST GIFT

"Moreover, Subhuti, when a bodhisattva practices generosity, he does not rely on any object—that is to say he does not rely on any form, sound, smell, taste, tactile object, or dharma—to practice generosity."

I think you already understand this sentence, even if you are hearing it for the first time. While working to relieve the suffering of others, you do it in the spirit of signlessness, not distinguishing between yourself and others. You do not base your work on the perception of a self, a person, a living being, or a life span. This spirit can be manifested in any act of generosity, practicing the precepts, endurance, energy, concentration, or understanding. Here, the Buddha uses generosity as an example.

There are three kinds of gifts: material resources, technical help or Dharma, and non-fear. In the *Heart Sutra*, Avalokita Bodhisattva offers us the gift of non-fear, or security. When traveling on the high seas, many Vietnamese boat people bring with them only a copy of the *Heart Sutra*. When we recite this prajñaparamita text with our full attention, we become fearless. Avalokita's gift to us is the greatest act of generosity one can offer.

When a bodhisattva practices generosity, he or she always does so in the spirit of fearlessness, not bound by the four wrong perceptions. In fact, the moment we are not imprisoned by the four erroneous perceptions, we are already in the world of non-fear. Erroneous perceptions arise because of our ignorance about the nature of perception. We do not see the true nature of the forms, sounds, smells, tastes, tactile objects, and objects of mind, and we are caught by them. If, on the other hand, we see someone who is hungry and offer him or her food without asking a lot of other questions or saying that we are practicing generosity, we are truly in the spirit of prajñaparamita and free from misperceptions.

People usually think that forms are stable and real, but according to the Buddha and modern science, form is made only of empty space. Any mass of matter, whether rock, iron, or wood, is composed of countless molecules which are, in turn, composed of countless atomic and subatomic particles, all of which are held together by electromagnetic and nuclear forces. Atoms are vast, empty spaces in which infinitely small particles—protons, electrons, neutrons, and so on—are in perpetual motion at enormous speeds. When we look deeply into matter, we see that it is like a beehive moving at a very great speed. Electrons travel around their nucleus at 300,000 kilometers per second. How erroneous was our concept of form! Physicists say that when they enter the world of atomic particles, they can see clearly that our conceptualized world is an illusion. The Buddha uses the image of a bubble to make it clear that there is space in matter, and he says the same is true of sounds, smells, tastes, tactile objects, and objects of mind. Due to our wrong perceptions about these six sense objects, we develop erroneous perceptions of a self, a person, a living being, and a life span. Therefore, while practicing generosity, we must go beyond our wrong perceptions and be free from them, not holding on to anything. If we take refuge in things that collapse easily, we too will collapse easily.

A meditation center, for example, is only a form. In our daily life we need forms, but we do not need to cling to them. We can study and practice meditation anywhere. If Plum Village were not here, we could go somewhere else. Once we see that, we become peaceful and fearless and are able to use the objects of our six senses freely. We know their true nature and are not their slaves. We do not feel more faith when they come together, and we do not feel less faith when they dissolve.

Bodhisattvas practice six methods for reaching the shore of enlightenment, known as the six paramitas—generosity, practicing the precepts, endurance, energy, concentration, and understanding. It is not correct to think that it is only possible to practice generosity when we have money. We can always offer others our peace and happiness. Many young people tell me, "Thây, I must get a job with a good salary because I want to help others." They study to become doctors or engineers, and studying takes most of their time now, so they do not have time to practice generosity. Then, after they become doctors or engineers, they are even busier and still do not have the time to practice generosity, even to themselves.

"That, Subhuti, is the spirit in which a bodhisattva should practice generosity, not relying on signs. Why? If a bodhisattva practices generosity without relying on signs, the happiness

*that results cannot be conceived of or measured. Subhuti, do
you think that the space in the Eastern Quarter can be measured?"*

"No, World-Honored One."

"Subhuti, can space in the Western, Southern, and Northern Quarters, above and below be measured?"

"No, World-Honored One."

*"Subhuti, if a bodhisattva does not rely on any concept when
practicing generosity, then the happiness that results from
that virtuous act is as great as space. It cannot be measured.
Subhuti, the bodhisattvas should let their minds dwell in the
teachings I have just given."*

The happiness that results from practicing generosity
without relying on signs is boundless. We often say that the
fruits of practice are peace and liberation. If we are washing
dishes and thinking of others who are enjoying themselves
doing nothing, we cannot enjoy washing the dishes. We may
have a few clean dishes afterwards, but our happiness is
smaller than one teaspoon. If, however, we wash the dishes
with a serene mind, our happiness will be boundless. This is
already liberation. The words in the sutra are very much related to our daily life.

5
SIGNLESSNESS

*"What do you think, Subhuti? Is it possible to grasp the
Tathagata by means of bodily signs?"*

*"No, World-Honored One. When the Tathagata speaks of
bodily signs, there are no signs being talked about."*

The Buddha said to Subhuti, "In a place where there is something that can be distinguished by signs, in that place there is deception. If you can see the signless nature of signs, then you can see the Tathagata."

Is it possible to grasp the Tathagata by the eighty signs of beauty or the thirty-two marks of a great person? Perceptions have signs as their object, and our perceptions are often inaccurate and sometimes quite erroneous. The accuracy of our perceptions depends on our insight. When we achieve insight, our knowledge is no longer based simply on perceptions, and we call this knowledge *prajña,* wisdom or understanding beyond signs.

In this passage, we encounter the dialectics of prajña-paramita. Our usual way of perceiving is according to the principle of identity: "A is A" and "A is not B." However, in this passage, Subhuti says, "A is not A." As we continue to study the *Diamond Sutra,* we will see many other sentences like this.

When the Buddha sees a rose, does he recognize it as a rose in the same way that we do? Of course he does. But before he says the rose is a rose, the Buddha has seen that the rose is not a rose. He has seen that it is made of non-rose elements, with no clear demarcation between the rose and those elements that are not the rose. When we perceive things, we generally use the sword of conceptualization to cut reality into pieces, saying, "This piece is A, and A cannot be B, C, or D." But when A is looked at in light of dependent co-arising, we see that A is comprised of B, C, D, and everything else in the universe. "A" can never exist by itself alone. When we look deeply into A, we see B, C, D, and so on. Once we understand that A is not just A, we understand the true nature of A and are qualified to say "A is A," or "A is not A." But until then, the A we see is just an illusion of the true A.

Look deeply at the one you love (or at someone you do not like at all!) and you will see that she is not herself alone. "She" includes her education, society, culture, heredity, parents, and all the things that contribute to her being. When we see that, we truly understand her. If she makes us unhappy, we can see that she did not intend to but that unfavorable conditions made her do it. To protect and cultivate the good qualities in her, we need to know how to protect and cultivate the elements outside of her, including ourselves, that make her fresh and lovely. If we are peaceful and pleasant, she too will be peaceful and pleasant.

If we look deeply into A and see that A is not A, we see A in its fullest flowering. At that time, love becomes true love, generosity becomes true generosity, practicing the precepts becomes truly practicing the precepts, and support becomes true support. This is the way the Buddha looks at a rose, and it is why he is not attached to the rose. When we are still caught in signs, we are still attached to the rose. A Chinese Zen master once said, "Before practicing Zen, mountains are mountains and rivers are rivers. While practicing Zen, mountains are no longer mountains and rivers are no longer rivers. After practicing, mountains are mountains again and rivers are rivers again." These are dialectics of prajña-paramita.

You know that monks and nuns are very much associated with signs. Their shaved heads, their robes, the way they walk, stand, sit, and lie down, are different from others, and, because of these signs, we can recognize them as monks and nuns. But some monks and nuns practice only for the form, so we cannot pass any judgments, positive or negative, based on signs. We must be able to see through the form in order to be in touch with the substance. Recognizing the Tathagata by means of the thirty-two marks or the eighty signs of beauty is dangerous, because Mara and the Wheel-Turning Kings (*cakravarti-raja*) also have the same signs. "Do not look for the Tathagata by means of bodily signs," the Buddha said. He also said, "Where there is sign, there is illusion." That is, when there is perception, there is deception. The substance of any perception is its sign. Our task is to practice until signs no longer deceive us and our perceptions become insight and understanding.

Tathagata is the true nature of life, wisdom, love, and happiness. Only when we can see the signless nature of signs do we have a chance of seeing the Tathagata. When we look at a rose without being caught by its signs, we see the nature of non-rose and therefore we begin to see the Tathagata in the rose. If we look into a pebble, a tree, or a child in this way, we also see the Tathagata in them. The *Diamond Sutra* defines Tathagata as "coming from nowhere and going nowhere," "showing no sign of coming and no sign of going, no sign of being and no sign of non-being, no sign of birth and no sign of death."

Before continuing, please read the first five sections of the sutra again. All of the essentials have been presented, and if you reread these sections, you will come to understand the meaning of *The Diamond that Cuts through Illusion*. Once you understand, you may find the *Diamond Sutra* like a piece of beautiful music. Without straining at all, the meaning will just enter you.

PART TWO
The Language of Non-Attachment

6

A ROSE IS NOT A ROSE

*The Venerable Subhuti said to the Buddha, "In times to come,
will there be people who, when they hear these teachings, have
real faith and confidence in them?"*

*The Buddha replied, "Do not speak that way, Subhuti. Five
hundred years after the Tathagata has passed away, there will
still be people who enjoy the happiness that comes from observing the precepts. When such people hear these words, they will
have faith and confidence that here is the truth. We should
know that such people have sown seeds not only during the lifetime of one Buddha, or even two, three, four, or five Buddhas,
but have, in truth, planted wholesome seeds during the lifetimes of tens of thousands of Buddhas."*

The Venerable Subhuti understands deeply what the Buddha has already explained. But he is concerned that those in
the future will not, since these teachings appear to contra-
dict common sense. It may not be difficult to understand the
teachings of the Buddha while he is alive, but 500 years after
he has passed away, those who hear these teachings may have
doubts. So the Buddha reassures Subhuti that there will still
be people in the future who are able to derive happiness
from following the precepts, and that these people, when
they hear the teaching of *The Diamond that Cuts through Illusion,* will accept these teachings just as Subhuti has ac-

cepted them. In fact, more than 2,000 years have passed
since the Buddha has entered parinirvana, and there are still
many people who practice the precepts and accept these
teachings.

In Buddhism, we often say that our mind is like a field,
and every time we do something wholesome or joyful, we
sow a Buddha seed in that field. In this passage, the Buddha
says that people who understand his teachings have planted
wholesome seeds during the lifetimes of tens of thousands
of Buddhas.

*"Anyone who, for only a second, gives rise to a pure and clear
confidence upon hearing these words of the Tathagata,
the Tathagata sees and knows that person, and he or she will
attain immeasurable happiness because of this understanding."*

There are two very important words in this sentence: see
and know. If, for one second, a person is confident about
these teachings, the Buddha will see and know that person.
To be seen and known by the Buddha is a great inspiration
and support for anyone on the path of practice. If we have
one close friend who can understand us and know our aspi-
rations, we feel greatly supported. A good friend does not
have to do much. He or she only needs to see us and know
that we are here, and we feel greatly encouraged. Imagine if
our friend is the Buddha!

This sentence in the *Diamond Sutra* became clear to me
one day several years ago as I was reading a poem I had written in 1967 for the brothers and sisters of the School of
Youth for Social Service. It was a pleasant surprise to have

insight into a sutra by reading or doing something else. I discovered that reading a sutra is like planting a tree inside our being. When we walk, look at the clouds, or read something else, the tree grows and it may reveal itself to us.

By 1967, the war in Vietnam had become so terrifying and destructive that many of the young social workers, monks, and nuns in the School of Youth for Social Service had to evacuate villagers even as the bombs were dropping. Already in exile, I received news from time to time that a brother or a sister of our school had been killed while doing this work. Neither the communists nor the anti-communists accepted our Buddhist movement. The communists thought that we were backed by the CIA, and the pro-American side suspected that we were communists. We would not accept the killing by either side. We only wanted reconciliation.

One evening, five young brothers were shot and four died. The one survivor told Sister Phuong that the killers had taken them to the riverbank, asked if they were members of the School of Youth for Social Service, and, when they said "Yes," said, "We are very sorry, but we have to kill you."

When I heard the news, I cried. A friend asked me, "Why do you cry? You are the commander-in-chief of a nonviolent army working for love. There are certain losses every army has to take. You are not taking the lives of people; you are saving lives. Even for warriors of love in a nonviolent army, casualties are inevitable."

I told him, "I am not a commander-in-chief. I am just a person. These young people joined the School in response to my call, and now they are dead. Of course I cry."

I wrote a poem for the brothers and sisters at the School and asked them to read it carefully. In that poem I told them never to look at anyone with hatred, even if they hate you, suppress you, kill you, or step on your life as if you were a wild plant or an insect. If you die because of violence, you must meditate on compassion in order to forgive those who killed you. The title of the poem is "Recommendation." Our only enemies are greed, violence, and fanaticism. When you die realizing this state of compassion, you are truly a child of the Awakened One. Before immolating herself to call for a cease-fire between the warring sides, my disciple, Sister Nhat Chi Mai, read the same poem into a cassette recorder and left the tape for her parents.

> Promise me, promise me this day,
>   promise me now,
> while the sun is shining above
> exactly at zenith, promise me
> even if people crush you
> under a mountain of hatred and violence,
> even if they walk on your life
> and crush you like a caterpillar,
> even if they amputate you,
> disembowel you,
> remember, brother,
> man is not our enemy.
> Only your compassion and
> your loving kindness are invincible,
> and without limit.
> Hatred can never respond
> to the beastliness in humankind.

One day when you are by yourself
facing cruelty,
your courage intact,
your calm eyes full of love,
even if no one knows of your smile,
blossoming as a flower in solitude and great pain,
those who love you will still see you
while traveling through a thousand worlds
of birth and death.
Alone again, I will go on
with my head bent down,
knowing that love has become eternal.
And on the long and difficult road,
the light of the sun and the moon
is still there
to guide my steps.

Even if you are dying in oppression, shame, and violence,
if you can smile with forgiveness, you have a great power.
When I was rereading these lines, I suddenly understood the
Diamond Sutra: "Your courage intact, your calm eyes full of
love, even if no one knows of your smile, blossoming as a
flower in solitude and great pain, those who love you will
still see you, while traveling through a thousand worlds of
birth and death." If you die with compassion in mind, you
are a torch lighting our path.

"Alone again, I will go on with my head bent down" in
order to see you, know you, remember you. Your love has
become eternal. Although the road is long and difficult, the
light of the sun and the moon is still there to guide my steps.
When there is a mature relationship between people, there

is always compassion and forgiveness. In our life, we need others to see and recognize us so that we feel supported. How much more do we need the Buddha to see us! On our path of service, there are moments of pain and loneliness, but when we know that the Buddha sees and knows us, we feel a great surge of energy and a firm determination to carry on.

"Why? Because that kind of person is not caught up in the idea of a self, a person, a living being, or a life span. They are not caught up in the idea of a dharma or the idea of a non-dharma. They are not caught up in the notion that this is a sign and that is not a sign. Why? If you are caught up in the idea of a dharma, you are also caught up in the ideas of a self, a person, a living being, and a life span. If you are caught up in the idea that there is no dharma, you are still caught up in the ideas of a self, a person, a living being, and a life span."

Sign here means concept. When we have a concept about something, its image appears within that concept. For example, when we have a concept of a table, we see an image of that table, but we must remember that our concept is not the thing itself. It is just our perception, which might in fact be very different from the table. A termite, for example, may perceive a table as a feast, and a physicist may perceive it as a mass of rapidly moving particles. Those of us on the path of Buddhist practice, because we have been practicing looking deeply, might have fewer erroneous views and our perceptions might be closer to being complete and true, but they are still perceptions.

In Buddhism, a dharma is commonly defined as any phenomenon that can maintain its unique characteristics and
not be mistaken for another phenomenon. Anger, sadness,
worry, and other psychological phenomena are called *citta
dharmas*. Chairs, tables, houses, mountaintops, rivers, and
other physical phenomena are called *rupa dharmas*.
Phenomena that are neither physical nor psychological,
such as gain, loss, being, and non-being, are classified as
cittaviprayukta-samskara dharmas. Phenomena that are not
conditioned by anything are called *asamskrita dharmas*.

According to the Sarvastivadin school of Buddhism, space
is an asamskrita dharma. It has a birthless and deathless nature and is not formed by anything. But this was just a way
for them to offer an example. In fact, space is made of such
things as time and consciousness and is, therefore, not really
an unconditioned dharma. The Sarvastivadins also call
"suchness" an unconditioned dharma, but if we look deeply,
we can see that suchness is not an unconditioned dharma
either. The concept of "suchness" exists because we have the
concept of "non-suchness." If we think that suchness is different from all other dharmas, our concept of suchness is
born from our concept of non-suchness. When there is
above, there is below; when there is inside, there is outside;
when there is permanence, there is impermanence. According to the law of relativity, our views are always defined by
their opposites.

In the dialectics of prajñaparamita, however, we have to
say the opposite: "Because this is not what it is, it really is
what it is." When we look into a dharma and see everything
that is not that dharma, we begin to see that dharma. There-

fore, we must not be bound to the concept of any dharma or even to the concept of non-dharma.

I am introducing the idea of non-dharma to help us go beyond the idea of dharma, but please do not get caught by the concept of non-dharma. When we see a rose, we know that the rose is a dharma. To avoid being caught by the concept "rose," we must remember that this rose cannot exist as a completely separate, independent entity but is made up only of non-rose elements. We know that rose is not a separate dharma, but once we leave behind the concept of a rose that can exist independently, we can be caught by the idea of non-rose. We must also be free from the concept of non-dharma.

In the dialectics of prajñaparamita, there are three stages: (1) A rose is (2) not a rose, therefore (3) it is a rose. The third rose is very different from the first. The notion "empty of emptiness" (shunyata) in the teaching of prajñaparamita aims at helping us be free from the concept of emptiness. Before practicing meditation, we see that mountains are mountains. When we start to practice, we see that mountains are no longer mountains. After practicing for a while, we see that mountains are again mountains. Now the mountains are very free. Our mind is still with the mountains, but it is no longer bound to anything. The mountains in the third stage are not the same as those in the first. In the third stage, the mountains reveal themselves freely, and we call this "true being." It is beyond being and non-being. The mountains are there in their wonderful presence, not as an illusion. When the Buddha sees a rose, the rose he sees is a miracle. It is the rose of true being. The rose that you and I see may be one of being, still full of conceptualizations. The notion of emptiness in the prajñaparamita literature is very deep. It goes beyond the illusory world of being and non-being, yes and no. It is called "true emptiness." True emptiness is not emptiness. True emptiness is true being.

When we dwell in the world of duality, we are conditioned by it. When we say, "My friend has passed away," and we cry, we are enslaved by the world of coming and going. The world of conditions is filled with erroneous views. It is only by learning to look deeply into the nature of things that we become free of the concepts of being and non-being and arrive in a world where such concepts as coming and going, existence and non-existence, birth and death, one and many, and above and below vanish. Once we are free, this world is still around us and inside us, but it is now the world of true emptiness. The principle of identity is at the top of the tree, but the world of true being is at the root. The principle of identity is the basis of the concept of self. Therefore, we have to break through the nets of both dharma and non-dharma and go beyond perceptions and non-perceptions.

"That is why we should not get caught up in dharmas or in the idea that dharmas do not exist. This is the hidden meaning when the Tathagata says, 'Bhikshus, you should know that all of the teachings I give to you are a raft.' All teachings must be abandoned, not to mention non-teachings."

The first sentence means that we should not get caught up in being or non-being, because both are illusory. When we no longer cling to these erroneous ideas, we arrive at the wondrous world of true emptiness.

At this point, the *Diamond Sutra* repeats what was said in the *Alaggadupama Sutta*. There the Buddha tells us that his teachings are like a raft that needs to be abandoned when we reach the other shore. The words "hidden meaning" are found only in the Sanskrit version, not in the Chinese one. When the Buddha offers teachings, it is possible that his listeners will cling to these teachings even after they are no longer appropriate or necessary. Listening to the teachings of the Buddha is like catching a dangerous snake. If you don't know how to do it, you might take hold of the tail first and the snake might turn around and bite you. If you know how to catch a snake, you will use a two-pronged stick to stop it, and then you will pick the snake up by the neck so that it cannot bite you. The same is true of the teachings of the Buddha—you can get hurt if you are unskillful. You must be careful not to get caught by the teachings. The ideas of emptiness, impermanence, and selflessness are extremely helpful, but if you use them without understanding them deeply and clearly, you can suffer and cause harm to others.

7
ENTERING THE OCEAN OF REALITY

"What do you think, Subhuti, has the Tathagata arrived at the highest, most fulfilled, awakened mind? Does the Tathagata give any teaching?"

The Venerable Subhuti replied, "As far as I have understood the Lord Buddha's teachings, there is no independently existing object of mind called the highest, most fulfilled, awakened mind, nor is there any independently existing teaching that the Tathagata gives. Why? The teachings that the Tathagata has realized and spoken of cannot be conceived of as separate, in-

dependent existences and therefore cannot be described. The Tathagata's teaching is not self-existent nor is it non-self-existent. Why? Because the noble teachers are only distinguished from others in terms of the unconditioned."

The Buddha is testing Subhuti to see if he understands what he has said concerning the dialectics of prajña-paramita. In answering the question whether the Tathagata has arrived at the highest, most fulfilled awakened mind and if there is any teaching that the Tathagata gives, Subhuti demonstrates his understanding by using the language of prajñaparamita. He goes on to explain that the teachings of the Tathagata can neither be grasped nor described. This is a very wise reply.

The Buddha has already explained these points, and now Subhuti repeats them in his own way by saying, "There is no independently existing object of mind called the highest, most fulfilled, awakened mind." If we say that there is a dharma called the highest, most fulfilled awakened mind, we are using the sword of conceptualization to slice out a piece of reality and call it the highest, most fulfilled, awakened mind. We should also be able to see the non-highest, non-most fulfilled, non-awakened mind just as we saw the non-rose elements while looking at a rose.

When Subhuti says that there is no independently existing object of mind called "the highest, most fulfilled, awakened mind," he means that what is called "the highest, most fulfilled, awakened mind" has no separate existence. Just as the rose cannot be separated from clouds, sun, soil, and rain, the teaching of the Buddha cannot be found outside of daily life. No dharma—not "the highest, most fulfilled, awakened mind," suchness, nirvana, Tathagata, a rose, eating a meal, washing the dishes, Subhuti, a friend, a house, a horse, or the teachings the Tathagata has realized—can be grasped or described.

The notion that things can exist independently of one another comes from the perception that they have a beginning and an end. But it is impossible to find the beginning or end of anything. When you look at your close friend, you may think that you understand her completely, but that is difficult because she is a river of reality. In every moment, dharmas that are not her enter and leave her. You cannot take hold of her. By observing her form, feelings, perceptions, mental formations, and consciousness, you can see that she is here sitting next to you, and she is elsewhere at the same time. She is in the present, the past, and the future. Your friend, the Tathagata, Subhuti, and the rose cannot be grasped because they have no beginning and no end. Their presence is deeply connected to all dharmas, all objects of mind in the universe.

When we practice Zen, we may be assigned the *kung-an* "What was your face before your parents were born?" We cannot grasp or describe this because it transcends forms. We have only our concepts, and we cannot grasp these dharmas through our perceptions. It is like trying to hold on to the air with our hand. The air slips out. This is why Subhuti said, "The teachings that the Tathagata has realized and spoken of cannot be conceived of as separate, independent existences and therefore cannot be described. The Tathagata's teaching is not self-existent nor is it non-self-existent." It is not correct to call the Tathagata's teaching a dharma, since by doing so we put it into a box, a pattern, and isolate it from other things. But saying it is not a dharma is also not correct, because it really is a dharma—not one that can be isolated but one that transcends all perceptions.

Then Subhuti says that the noble teachers can be distinguished from others only in terms of the unconditioned. "Noble teachers" is a translation of the Sanskrit term *aryapudgala. Arya* means honor. *Pudgala* means person. Aryapudgala are those who have attained the status of "Stream-Enterer" *(sotapatti-phala),* "Once-Returner" *(sakadagami-phala),* "Never-Returner *(anagami-phala),* or "the one who is free from craving and rebirth" *(arhat). Asamskrita dharmas* are unconditioned. They transcend all concepts. The noble teachers are liberated. They are distinguished from others because they are in touch with and realize the unconditioned dharmas. They are no longer imprisoned by forms and concepts.

This section of the sutra shows that all dharmas are without form and transcend conceptual knowledge. When we realize the suchness of all dharmas, we are freed from our conceptual prisons. In daily life, we usually use our conceptual knowledge to grasp reality. But this is impossible. Meditation aims at breaking through all conceptual limitations and barriers so that we can move freely in the boundless ocean of reality.

8
NON-ATTACHMENT

"What do you think, Subhuti? If someone were to fill the 3,000 chiliocosms with the seven precious treasures as an act of generosity, would that person bring much happiness by this virtuous act?"

The Venerable Subhuti replied, "Yes, World-Honored One. It is because the very natures of virtue and happiness are not virtue and happiness that the Tathagata is able to speak about virtue and happiness."

Chiliocosm comes from two Greek words: *chilioi,* meaning "a thousand," and *kosmos,* meaning "universe." Three thousand chiliocosms means an innumerable number of universes. The Buddha asks, "If someone were to fill the 3,000 chiliocosms with the seven precious treasures as an act of generosity, would that person bring much happiness by this virtuous act?" Subhuti replies, "Yes," and goes on to show the Buddha that he is not confined by language. Aware that there are no separate objects of mind called "virtue" or "happiness," Subhuti is no longer imprisoned by words and therefore can use them without any harm. But if we do not see the nature of interbeing implied in each word, they can be a kind of attachment or imprisonment. We have to use words in a way that they do not enslave us. This is why the Buddha is giving us *The Diamond that Cuts through Illusion.*

The Buddha said, "On the other hand, if there is someone who accepts these teachings and puts them into practice, even if only a gatha of four lines, and explains them to someone else, the happiness brought about by this virtuous act far exceeds the happiness brought about by giving the seven precious treasures."

The happiness brought about by this virtuous act is boundless. It is the utmost, unconditioned emancipation, not merely an accumulation of conditioned happinesses.

"Why? Because, Subhuti, all Buddhas and the dharma of the highest, most fulfilled, awakened mind of all Buddhas arise from these teachings."

This remarkable proclamation embraces the notion that prajña, understanding, is the mother of all buddhas and bodhisattvas.

"Subhuti, what is called Buddhadharma is everything that is not Buddhadharma."

Those who bring Buddhist practice to the West should do so in this spirit. Since Buddhism is not yet known to most Westerners, the essence of Buddhism won't have much chance to blossom in the West if the teachings emphasize form too much. If you think that the teachings of Buddhism are completely separate from the other teachings in your society, that is a big mistake. When I travel in the West to share the teachings of Buddhism, I often remind people that there are spiritual values in Western culture and tradition—Judaism, Islam, and Christianity—that share the essence of Buddhism. When you look deeply into your culture and tradition, you will discover many beautiful spiritual values. They are not called Buddhadharma, but they are really Buddhadharma in their content.

In his last meal, for example, Jesus held up a piece of bread and shared it with his students, saying, "Friends, eat this bread which is my flesh. I offer it to you." When he poured the wine, he said, "Here is my blood. I offer it to you. Drink it." Many years ago, when I met Cardinal Danielou in Paris, I told him, "I think Lord Jesus was teaching his students the practice of mindfulness." In our life, we eat and drink many times a day, but while doing so, our mind is usually wandering elsewhere, and what we really eat are our worries, thoughts, and anxieties. Eating in mindfulness is to be in touch with life. Jesus spoke the way he did so that his students would *really* eat the bread. The Last Supper was a mindfulness meal. If the disciples could pierce through their distractions and eat one piece of bread in the present moment with their whole being, isn't that Buddhadharma? Words like "mindfulness" or "meditation" may not have been used, but the fact that thirteen people were sitting and eating together in mindfulness is surely the practice of Buddhism. Vietnamese King Tran Nhan Tong once said that eating a meal, drinking water, and using the toilet are all Buddhadharma. Buddhadharma is not something different from so-called non-Buddhadharma.

The *Diamond Sutra* is not difficult to understand, although it may sound strange until you get used to this kind of language. It also may seem repetitive, but if you read it carefully, you will find something new in every sentence. Moreover, the *Diamond Sutra* helps us sow many wholesome seeds into our consciousness, so when a similar thought is repeated, good seeds are sown into our store consciousness *(alaya vijñana)*. In teaching the *Diamond Sutra*, the Buddha is training Subhuti how to use the language of non-attachment. As we become conversant in this language, we are able to develop our deepest understanding.

PART THREE

The Answer Is in the Question

9
DWELLING IN PEACE

"What do you think, Subhuti? Does a Stream-Enterer think, 'I have attained the fruit of Stream-Entry.'?"

Subhuti replied, "No, World-Honored One. Why? Stream-Enterer means to enter the stream, but in fact there is no stream to enter. One does not enter a stream that is form, nor a stream that is sound, smell, taste, touch, or object of mind. That is what we mean when we say entering a stream."

According to traditional Buddhism, Stream-Entry is the first of the four fruits of the practice. When you become a Stream-Enterer, you enter the stream of awakened mind, which always flows into the ocean of emancipation. Is that stream a dharma that exists independently from other dharmas? Subhuti's reply is very much in the language of the dialectics of prajñaparamita.

"What do you think, Subhuti? Does a Once-Returner think, 'I have attained the fruit of Once-Returning.'?"

Subhuti replied, "No, World-Honored One. Why? Once-Returner means to go and return once more, but in truth there is no going just as there is no returning. That is what we mean when we say Once-Returner."

The nature of all dharmas is neither coming nor going. There is no point in space from which they come, and there is no point in space to which they go. They reveal themselves only when conditions are sufficient. When conditions are insufficient, they are latent. The same is true of human beings. According to the traditional definition, a Once-Returner is a person who, after death, will return to the cycle of birth and death just one more time before realizing the fruit of Arhatship (no birth, no death). But in truth, we come from nowhere and we go nowhere. That is why we say such a person is a Once-Returner.

"What do you think, Subhuti? Does a Non-Returner think like this, 'I have attained the fruit of No-Return.'?"

Subhuti replied, "No, World-Honored One. Why? No-Return means not to return to this world, but in fact there cannot be any Non-Returning. That is what we mean when we say Non-Returner."

Those who realize the fruit of never returning do not return after this life to this world. It is said that they go to another world to practice until they realize the fruit of Arhatship. Once again, Subhuti applies the language of the dialectics of prajñaparamita. He says that the idea of returning is already illusory, much less the idea of non-returning.

"What do you think, Subhuti? Does an Arhat think like this, 'I have attained the fruit of Arhatship.'?"

Subhuti replied, "No, World-Honored One. Why? There is no separately existing thing that can be called Arhat. If an Arhat gives rise to the thought that he has attained the fruit of

Arhatship, then he is still caught up in the idea of a self, a person, a living being, and a life span. World-Honored One, you have often said that I have attained the concentration of peaceful abiding and that in the community, I am the Arhat who has most transformed need and desire. World-Honored One, if I were to think that I had attained the fruit of Arhatship, you certainly would not have said that I love to dwell in the concentration of peaceful abiding."

Arana means the absence of struggle. Subhuti is well known throughout the Buddha's community as someone who likes to dwell in the practice of *arana,* peaceful abiding. He has no wish to compete with anyone. He is regarded as an Arhat, one who has transformed all afflictions and desires. Because Subhuti is not caught by the idea that he has attained the fruit of Arhatship, he is truly an Arhat. At Plum Village, we eat vegetarian food without thinking of ourselves as vegetarians. This is the essence of non-action or formlessness. Because Subhuti practices non-action, he is praised by the World-Honored One as a disciple who loves to dwell in peace.

10
CREATING A FORMLESS PURE LAND

The Buddha asked Subhuti, "In ancient times when the Tathagata practiced under Buddha Dipankara, did he attain anything?"

Subhuti answered, "No, World-Honored One. In ancient times when the Tathagata was practicing under Buddha Dipankara, he did not attain anything."

"What do you think, Subhuti? Does a bodhisattva create a serene and beautiful Buddha field?"

"No, World-Honored One. Why? To create a serene and beautiful Buddha field is not in fact creating a serene and beautiful Buddha field. That is why it is called creating a serene and beautiful Buddha field."

Upon attaining enlightenment, all Buddhas and bodhisattvas open a new world for people on the path of realization who want to study and practice with them. Every Buddha creates a pure land as a practice center. A pure land is a fresh, beautiful place where people are happy and peaceful. Creating a pure land is called "setting up a serene and beautiful Buddha field." Teachers and students work together to make such a place beautiful, pleasant, and fresh, so that many people can go there to live and practice. The greater their power of awakening and peace, the more pleasant is their pure land.

Amitabha Buddha has a Pure Land in the Western Paradise. Akshobya Buddha has a place called Wondrous Joy. After a period of practice, if you have some attainment and peace, you may wish to share them with others and establish a small practice community. But this should always be done in the spirit of formlessness. Do not be bound by the practice center you establish. "To create a serene and beautiful Buddha field is not in fact creating a serene and beautiful Buddha field" means to do so in the spirit of formlessness. Do not let yourself be devoured by your Buddha field or you will suffer. Do not allow yourself to be burnt out in the process of setting up a practice center.

The Buddha said, "So, Subhuti, all the bodhisattva maha-
sattvas should give rise to a pure and clear intention in this
spirit. When they give rise to this intention, they should not
rely on forms, sounds, smells, tastes, tactile objects, or objects
of mind. They should give rise to an intention with their minds
not dwelling anywhere."

Not dwelling anywhere means not relying on anything.
Giving rise to an intention means having the wish to attain
the highest awakening. Relying on forms, sounds, smells,
tastes, tactile objects, and objects of minds means being
caught by perceptions, ideas, and concepts. In Section Two
of this sutra, the first question Subhuti asked the Buddha
was, "If sons and daughters of good families want to give rise
to the highest, most fulfilled, awakened mind, what should
they rely on and what should they do to master their thinking?" This passage is the Buddha's answer.

"Subhuti, if there were someone with a body as big as Mount
Sumeru, would you say that his was a large body?"
    Subhuti answered, "Yes, World-Honored One, very large.
Why? What the Tathagata says is not a large body, that is
known as a large body."

The word "body" is a translation of the Sanskrit word
atmabhava, not the word *kaya*. Mount Sumeru is the king of
all mountains. In this paragraph, the teacher and his student
are still using the language of dialectics of prajñaparamita.
When the Buddha asks, "Would you say that his was a large
body?" Subhuti answers, "Very large," because he understands clearly the Buddha's language. He is aware that the

Buddha says "large" because he is free of the concepts of large and small. If we are aware of the way the Buddha uses words, we will not be caught by any of his words. The teacher is important, the director of the practice center is important, but if the idea of being important becomes an obstacle for the teaching and the practice, then the meaning will be lost.

11

THE SAND IN THE GANGES

"Subhuti, if there were as many Ganges Rivers as the number of grains of sand in the Ganges, would you say that the number of grains of sand in all those Ganges Rivers is very many?"

Subhuti answered, "Very many indeed, World-Honored One. If the number of Ganges Rivers were huge, how much more so the number of grains of sand in all those Ganges Rivers."

"Subhuti, now I want to ask you this: if a daughter or son of good family were to fill the 3,000 chiliocosms with as many precious jewels as the number of grains of sand in all the Ganges Rivers as an act of generosity, would that person bring much happiness by her virtuous act?"

Subhuti replied, "Very much, World-Honored One."

The Buddha said to Subhuti, "If a daughter or son of a good family knows how to accept, practice, and explain this sutra to others, even if it is a gatha of four lines, the happiness that results from this virtuous act would be far greater."

The number of grains of sand in the Ganges means a quantity that cannot be reached using mathematics. If one were to fill the 3,000 chiliocosms with as many precious jewels as there are grains of sand in the Ganges as an act of generosity, the happiness that is brought about by this virtuous act would still be less than the happiness brought about by accepting, practicing, and explaining the *Diamond Sutra*. The happiness resulting from the study and practice of *The Diamond that Cuts through Illusion* is so great that it has become an object of worship, as can be seen in the next section of the sutra.

12

EVERY LAND IS A HOLY LAND

"Furthermore, Subhuti, any plot of land on which this sutra is proclaimed, even if only one gatha of four lines, will be a land where gods, men, and asuras will come to make offerings just as they make offerings to a stupa of the Buddha. If the plot of land is regarded as that sacred, how much more so the person who practices and recites this sutra. Subhuti, you should know that that person attains something rare and profound. Wherever this sutra is kept is a sacred site enshrining the presence of the Buddha or one of the Buddha's great disciples."

Any ground on which this sutra, even one verse of four lines, is proclaimed is a holy land that is worthy of offerings by gods, men, and asuras, as sacred and precious as any stupa of the Buddha's relics. If the plot of land is sacred, how much more so the person who practices and recites the sutra, for that means the sutra has penetrated into the flesh, soul, and life of that person. That person is now worthy of offerings by gods, men, and asuras.

In 1963 in Saigon, the bodhisattva Thich Quang Duc immolated himself in order to awaken our country's dictators.

When poet Vu Hoang Chuong visualized the ground on which Thich Quang Duc had sat, he knew that that ground was holy ground, and he said, "The place you sit has become an eternal *chef d'œuvre,* your compassion shines from the heart of invisibility." Vu Hoang Chuong may not have studied the *Diamond Sutra,* but he arrived at the same insight. When a person uses his body to save the lives of his fellow beings, his compassion can transform the ground on which he sits into a holy ground. Even though no statue or stupa is there, it is still truly a holy ground and should be considered a place for worship.

13
THE DIAMOND THAT CUTS THROUGH ILLUSION

After that, Subhuti asked the Buddha, "What should this sutra be called and how should we act regarding its teachings?"

The Buddha replied, "This sutra should be called The Diamond that Cuts through Illusion *because it has the capacity to cut through all illusions and afflictions and bring us to the shore of liberation. Please use this title and practice according to its deepest meaning. Why? What the Tathagata has called the highest, transcendent understanding is not, in fact, the highest, transcendent understanding. That is why it is truly the highest, transcendent understanding."*

The Buddha asked, "What do you think, Subhuti? Is there any dharma that the Tathagata teaches?"

Subhuti replied, "The Tathagata has nothing to teach, World-Honored One."

"What do you think, Subhuti? Are there many particles of dust in the 3,000 chiliocosms?"

"Very many, World-Honored One."

"Subhuti, the Tathagata says that these particles of dust are not particles of dust. That is why they are truly particles of dust. And what the Tathagata calls chiliocosms are not in fact chiliocosms. That is why they are called chiliocosms."

"What do you think, Subhuti? Can the Tathagata be recognized by the possession of the thirty-two marks?"

The Venerable Subhuti replied, "No, World-Honored One. Why? Because what the Tathagata calls the thirty-two marks are not essentially marks and that is why the Tathagata calls them the thirty-two marks."

"Subhuti, if as many times as there are grains of sand in the Ganges a son or daughter of a good family gives up his or her life as an act of generosity and if another daughter or son of a good family knows how to accept, practice, and explain this sutra to others, even if only a gatha of four lines, the happiness resulting from explaining this sutra is far greater."

Subhuti asks what this sutra should be called and how we should practice its teachings, and the Buddha answers that it should be called *The Diamond that Cuts through Illusion.* A diamond has the capacity to cut through all ignorance and afflictions. He also says that we should practice in an intelligent way, that we should learn to look deeply so that we will realize that even transcendent understanding is not an independently existing dharma and that his teaching has no separate nature. That is why Subhuti says, "The Tathagata has nothing to teach."

If someone were to grind the 3,000 chiliocosms into dust, these particles of dust would be very, very many. We should look deeply into the concepts of "many" and "chiliocosms" with the eye of transcendent understanding if we want to avoid being caught by these concepts. The same is true of the concepts of "dust" and "thirty-two marks." Although such words are used, we should not be caught by them. If some-one were to accept, practice, and explain these teachings, even if only one verse of four lines, the happiness resulting from this would be far greater than the happiness that would result from any other virtuous act. Because the practice of non-attachment as it is taught in the sutra can liberate us completely from wrong views, the happiness that results from this practice is far greater than any kind of happiness. Virtuous acts still based on the ground of self, person, living being, and life span may bring some happiness, but com-pared to the happiness of true liberation, it is still quite small. When a person is absolutely free from wrong views, his or her actions will greatly benefit the world. The practice of *The Diamond that Cuts through Illusion* is thus the basis for all meaningful action.

14

ABIDING IN NON-ABIDING

When he had heard this much and penetrated deeply into its significance, the Venerable Subhuti was moved to tears. He said, "World-Honored One, you are truly rare in this world. Since the day I attained the eyes of understanding, thanks to the guidance of the Buddha, I have never before heard teach-ings so deep and wonderful as these. World-Honored One, if someone hears this sutra, has pure and clear confidence in it, and arrives at insight into the truth, that person will realize the rarest kind of virtue. World-Honored One, that insight into the truth is essentially not insight. That is what the Tathagata calls insight into the truth.

"World-Honored One, today it is not difficult for me to hear this wonderful sutra, have confidence in it, understand it, accept it, and put it into practice. But in the future, in 500 years, if there is someone who can hear this sutra, have confidence in it, understand it, accept it, and put it into practice, then certainly the existence of someone like that will be great and rare. Why? That person will not be dominated by the idea of a self, a person, a living being, or a life span. Why? The idea of a self is not an idea, and the ideas of a person, a living being, and a life span are not ideas either. Why? Buddhas are called Buddhas because they are free of ideas."

When he heard this much and penetrated deeply into its significance, the Venerable Subhuti was moved to tears. Hearing something so profound or seeing a view so beautiful, we too may be moved to tears of happiness. Then Subhuti says, "Since the day I attained the eyes of understanding, I have never before heard teachings so deep and wonderful as these." The eyes of understanding mentioned here are not yet the eyes of the deepest, all embracing understanding of a Buddha. They are only the eyes of an Arhat. This means that Subhuti is beginning to see things more deeply after hearing this much of the *Diamond Sutra*.

If someone hears this sutra, has confidence in it, and arrives at insight into the truth, that person will have pure, clear, and stable confidence without questions or doubts. *The Diamond that Cuts through Illusion* came into existence 500 years after the Buddha entered nirvana. This sutra is difficult to understand because what is said is contrary to the common perceptions of people. Therefore, anyone who can understand the *Diamond Sutra*, at any time, should know that he or she is of a very rare nature.

Subhuti goes on to say, "The idea of a self is not an idea, and the ideas of a person, a living being, and a life span are not ideas either. Why? Buddhas are called Buddhas because they are free of ideas." The English word "view" is actually closer to the Chinese character used here than the word "idea," although views themselves are ideas or perceptions. Any perception has two parts: a viewer (subject) and that which is being viewed (object). A self view, a person view, a living-being view, and a life span view are all objects of perception. They are neither independently existing nor permanent. Like everything else, they are of the nature of interbeing. The last line is a powerful statement: "Buddhas are called Buddhas because they are free of ideas."

The Buddha said to Subhuti, "That is quite right. If someone hears this sutra and is not terrified or afraid, he or she is rare. Why? Subhuti, what the Tathagata calls paramaparamita, *the highest transcendence, is not essentially the highest transcendence, and that is why it is called the highest transcendence.*

"Subhuti, the Tathagata has said that what is called transcendent endurance is not transcendent endurance. That is why it is called transcendent endurance. Why? Subhuti, thousands of lifetimes ago when my body was cut into pieces by King Kalinga, I was not caught in the idea of a self, a person, a living being, or a life span. If, at that time, I had been caught up in any of those ideas, I would have felt anger and ill-will against the king."

The Buddha uses transcendent endurance, one of the six paramitas, as an example of the spirit of deep understanding. According to the *Prajñaparamita* (known as the *"Mother of all Buddhas") Sutras*, prajñaparamita is the clay pot that contains all the other paramitas. If the clay has not been fired properly, liquids stored in it will gradually leak out. That is why prajñaparamita is the very foundation. The Buddha was able to practice transcendent endurance because he had attained transcendent understanding, prajñaparamita.

Thousands of lifetimes ago, when his body was cut to pieces by King Kalinga, the bodhisattva who was to become the Buddha was able not to get angry because he already had transcendent understanding, that is, he was not caught up in views. He was not caught up in the idea of a self, a person, a living being, or a life span. If the bodhisattva had still been caught up in views, he would have had ill-will against the king and would not have succeeded. We can see that what is called transcendent endurance is, in fact, not only transcendent endurance. It is, at the same time, transcendent generosity and observing the precepts, as well as everything else that is not transcendent endurance. Just as a rose is not just a rose, transcendent endurance cannot exist independently of the other five paramitas. With this understanding, we can call it transcendent endurance. As we begin to follow the Buddha's reasoning, we can see why he talks about transcendent endurance in order to teach about prajñaparamita, transcendent understanding.

"I also remember in ancient times, for 500 lifetimes, I practiced transcendent endurance by not being caught up in the idea of a self, a person, a living being, or a life span. So, Subhuti, when

*a bodhisattva gives rise to the unequalled mind of awakening,
he has to give up all ideas. He cannot rely on forms when he
gives rise to that mind, nor on sounds, smells, tastes, tactile
objects, or objects of mind. He can only give rise to that mind
that is not caught up in anything."*

A mind that still relies on one thing does not abide in still-
ness. That is why the Buddha always says that the bodhisattva should not rely on form to practice generosity. In
order to really benefit living beings, the bodhisattva practices generosity without relying on anything. In this section,
the Buddha repeats what he has already said several times in
this sutra: A mind that does not rely on anything is not
caught by forms, sounds, smells, tastes, tactile objects, or
objects of mind. When we take refuge in something that is
changing, we can never have peace. We need to abide in what
is stable. All objects of our six senses are conditioned and
continuously changing. If we abide in them, we will not have
stability.

Today, throughout the world, many single parents are trying to raise children by themselves. It is difficult, and many
of them are not at peace. They are working hard to give up
the idea of needing a partner so they can just rely on themselves. In the past they may have relied on someone who
lacked stability, and their relationship fell apart. But I know
that many of them still wish to find another person to rely
on.

There are many stable things we can rely on—the earth,
the air, the Buddha, the Dharma, the Sangha. It is always
best to take refuge in something that is stable. Otherwise, if
the object of our refuge changes or falls apart, we too may

fall apart. The most stable is to abide in the non-abiding. Before Vietnamese Dhyana master Van Hanh passed away, he asked his disciples, "Where do you abide, my students? I abide in neither abiding nor non-abiding." A mind that abides in anything, ultimately, cannot have peace. That is why the Buddha often tells the bodhisattvas not to rely on form to practice generosity. Because they truly wish to benefit other beings, the bodhisattvas practice generosity in this spirit.

"The Tathagata has said that all notions are not notions and that all living beings are not living beings. Subhuti, the Tathagata is one who speaks of things as they are, speaks what is true, and speaks in accord with reality. He does not speak deceptively or to please people. Subhuti, if we say that the Tathagata has realized a teaching, that teaching is neither graspable nor deceptive.

"Subhuti, a bodhisattva who still depends on notions to practice generosity is like someone walking in the dark. He will not see anything. But when a bodhisattva does not depend on notions to practice generosity, he is like someone with good eyesight walking under the bright light of the sun. He can see all shapes and colors.

"Subhuti, if in the future there is any daughter or son of good family who has the capacity to accept, read, and put into practice this sutra, the Tathagata will see that person with his eyes of understanding. The Tathagata will know that person, and that person will realize the measureless, limitless fruit of her or his virtuous act."

The Buddha is saying that the truth he has realized is not what we generally think it is. It lies in the middle way, which is beyond the idea of graspable and the idea of deceptive. We should understand this in light of the teaching of the raft given earlier. The raft is to help us cross over to the other shore. It is a wonderful, even necessary instrument. But we should use the raft in an intelligent way. We should not cling to it or carry it on our back after we are done with it. The teaching is to help us, not to be possessed by us. It is not meant to deceive us, but we may be deceived by it because of our own way of clinging to it. The finger that is pointing to the moon is not the moon. We need the finger to see the moon. The finger is not deceiving us, but if we cling to it, we may miss the moon and feel that we have been deceived by the finger.

As long as we are still caught up in ideas and signs, we are blinded by them. When we walk in the dark, we cannot see reality as it is. But when we are free of the concepts of signs—of forms, sounds, smells, tastes, tactile objects, and objects of mind—we are like those with perfect vision walking in the midday sun. We can see directly into the world of "wondrous reality," where everything reveals its true nature.

15
GREAT DETERMINATION

"Subhuti, if on the one hand, a daughter or son of a good family gives up her or his life in the morning as many times as there are grains of sand in the Ganges as an act of generosity, and gives as many again in the afternoon and as many again in the evening, and continues doing so for countless ages; and if, on the other hand, another person listens to this sutra with com-

plete confidence and without contention, that person's happiness will be far greater. But the happiness of one who writes this sutra down, receives, recites, and explains it to others cannot be compared.

"In summary, Subhuti, this sutra brings about boundless virtue and happiness that cannot be conceived or measured. If there is someone capable of receiving, practicing, reciting, and sharing this sutra with others, the Tathagata will see and know that person, and he or she will have inconceivable, indescribable, and incomparable virtue. Such a person will be able to shoulder the highest, most fulfilled, awakened career of the Tathagata. Why? Subhuti, if one is content with the small teachings, if he or she is still caught up in the idea of a self, a person, a living being, or a life span, he or she will not be able to listen, receive, recite, and explain this sutra to others. Subhuti, any place this sutra is found is a place where gods, men, and asuras will come to make offerings. Such a place is a shrine and should be venerated with formal ceremonies, circumambulations, and offerings of flowers and incense."

Please take note of the phrase "writes down" towards the end of the first paragraph. For more than 500 years, the texts of the Canon were transmitted orally. They were not written on palm leaves until the first century B.C.E. It was in that period, perhaps twenty or thirty years earlier, that *The Diamond that Cuts through Illusion* made its appearance.

In this section, the Buddha mentions the "small teachings." These small teachings are authentic teachings of the Buddha, but they are not his most profound ones. The Buddha's teachings can be seen as a house with an outer room and many inner rooms. If we stay in the outer room, we may only benefit from a table, a chair, and a few other small comforts. We may have come to the Buddha with the intention of relieving our most profound suffering, but if we are content to stay in this outer room, we will obtain only minimal relief. When we feel calm enough, we may open the door and go further into the inner rooms of the Buddha's house. We will discover many precious gems and treasures in these rooms. As the heirs of the Buddha, we should make the effort to receive his most precious gifts. They can provide us with the energy and determination to help many other people. These gifts are called the "great Dharma." The great Dharma is the heart of a bodhisattva. "Small teachings" here means the teachings offered only to shravakas and not to bodhisattvas.

16

THE LAST EPOCH

"Furthermore, Subhuti, if a son or daughter of good family, while reciting and practicing this sutra, is disdained or slandered, his or her misdeeds committed in past lives, including those that could bring about an evil destiny, will be eradicated, and he or she will attain the fruit of the most fulfilled, awakened mind. Subhuti, in ancient times before I met Buddha Dipankara, I had made offerings to and had been attendant of all 84,000 multi-millions of buddhas. If someone is able to receive, recite, study, and practice this sutra in the last epoch, the happiness brought about by this virtuous act is hundreds of thousands times greater than that which I brought about in ancient times. In fact, such happiness cannot be conceived or compared with anything, even mathematically. Such happiness is immeasurable."

"Disdain" and "slander" are translations of the Sanskrit word *parimuta*. This paragraph gives us the impression that even as the *Diamond Sutra* was being written down, it was already being condemned by some who probably criticized these teachings as not being the original words of the Buddha. Those who were reciting this sutra were probably also being denigrated, so right in the sutra it says that if anyone maintains confidence in these teachings, their study and practice will give rise to immeasurable virtue and happiness—their misdeeds from the past will be absolved, including those that could bring them to the three evil realms of hell-beings, hungry ghosts, and animals, and they will attain the highest, most fulfilled, awakened mind.

Today, Mahayana Buddhism has become a tradition, and the number of people who condemn these teachings is relatively few. But during that period, after a sutra like this appeared, studying, reciting, practicing, copying, and spreading it could make you a target for attack. So the Buddha offers an example that in ancient times, before he met Buddha Dipankara, he had already made offerings to and had been attendant of 84,000 of multi-millions of buddhas, yet the happiness brought about by these virtuous acts was far less than the virtue generated by someone who will be born at the end of the last epoch who studies and practices this sutra. "The end of the last epoch" means the time when the deepest teachings of the Buddha will not have a chance to spread anymore.

"Subhuti, the happiness resulting from the virtuous act of a son or daughter of good family who receives, recites, studies, and practices this sutra in the last epoch will be so great that if I

were to explain it now in detail, some people would become suspicious and disbelieving, and their minds might become disoriented. Subhuti, you should know that the meaning of this sutra is beyond conception and discussion. Likewise, the fruit resulting from receiving and practicing this sutra is beyond conception and discussion."

In the *Ekottara Agama,* the Buddha lists four things that can neither be conceived of nor explained: (1) the virtue of a Buddha, (2) the state of a person dwelling in concentration, (3) the notions of karma and consequence, and (4) the origin of the universe. Anyone who thinks, "I have already explained this sutra thoroughly and completely," has not really understood this sutra. Studying and practicing *The Diamond that Cuts through Illusion* will result in the kind of peace, joy, and action that will have the power to change the world. The happiness it produces is beyond all conception and discussion.

Even if we are only washing dishes, the peace and joy experienced from the practice of the sutra while washing the dishes cannot be described—they are beyond conception and discussion. The merit produced by washing dishes will be immeasurable.

17

THE ANSWER IS IN THE QUESTION

At that time, the Venerable Subhuti said to the Buddha, "World-Honored One, may I ask you again that if daughters or sons of good family want to give rise to the highest, most fulfilled, awakened mind, what should they rely on and what should they do to master their thinking?"

The Buddha replied, "Subhuti, a good son or daughter who wants to give rise to the highest, most fulfilled, awakened mind should do it in this way: 'We must lead all beings to the shore of awakening, but, after these beings have become liberated, we do not, in truth, think that a single being has been liberated.' Why is this so? Subhuti, if a bodhisattva is still caught up in the idea of a self, a person, a living being or a life span, that person is not an authentic bodhisattva. Why is that?

"Subhuti, in fact, there is no independently existing object of mind called the highest, most fulfilled, awakened mind. What do you think, Subhuti? In ancient times, when the Tathagata was living with Buddha Dipankara, did he attain anything called the highest, most fulfilled, awakened mind?"

"No, World-Honored One. According to what I understand from the teachings of the Buddha, there is no attaining of anything called the highest, most fulfilled, awakened mind."

The Buddha said, "Right you are, Subhuti. In fact, there does not exist the so-called highest, most fulfilled, awakened mind that the Tathagata attains. Because if there had been any such thing, Buddha Dipankara would not have predicted of me, 'In the future, you will come to be a Buddha called Shakyamuni.' This prediction was made because there is, in fact, nothing that can be attained that is called the highest, most fulfilled, awakened mind. Why? Tathagata means the suchness of all things (dharmas). Someone would be mistaken to say that the Tathagata has attained the highest, most fulfilled, awakened mind since there is not any highest, most fulfilled, awakened mind to be attained. Subhuti, the highest, most fulfilled, awakened mind that the Tathagata has attained is neither graspable nor elusive. This is why the Tathagata has said, 'All dharmas are Buddhadharma.' What are called all dharmas are, in fact, not all dharmas. That is why they are called all dharmas."

Here the Buddha repeats what was said in the beginning of the sutra to help water the seeds that were sown in our consciousness at that time. There are things in this passage that are already clear, but certain things still need to be reviewed.

Tathagata means suchness, the suchness of all objects of mind, of all dharmas. All objects of mind have their outer appearance which is called "illusory sign." When our mind holds on to this illusory form, it makes an "erroneous perception." The concepts of birth and death, high and low, many and one are all erroneous. If we can break through all erroneous perceptions and penetrate directly into the true nature of all objects of mind, we will be in touch with suchness. To be in touch with the suchness of all dharmas is to see the Tathagata, and to see the Tathagata is to be in touch with the suchness of all dharmas. The Tathagata *is* the suchness of all objects of mind.

"Someone would be mistaken to say that the Tathagata has attained the highest, most fulfilled, awakened mind since there is not any highest, most fulfilled, awakened mind to be attained." When we think that we have something now that we did not have before, we are caught up in the ideas of having and not having, and we still do not see suchness. Through the prism of our erroneous perceptions, we see being and non-being, gain and loss, attainment and non-attainment, and we fail to see the suchness of all dharmas.

"Subhuti, the highest, most fulfilled, awakened mind that the Tathagata has attained is neither graspable nor elusive."

We may think that birth and death, one and many, and gain and loss are erroneous but that suchness is true. But suchness is free of all concepts like true and false, graspable and deceptive. If we say that other objects of mind are deceptive but that suchness is not deceptive, that too is a mistake. Like all concepts, deceptive and not deceptive are wrong perceptions and are not at all related to suchness. This is why the Tathagata can say, "All dharmas are Buddhadharma."

A Zen master said, "Eating, drinking, and going to the toilet are all Buddhadharma." Because Buddhadharma is made of non-Buddhadharma elements, Buddhadharma cannot be found outside of non-Buddhadharma. This is explained clearly in the *Ratnakuta Sutra*. Those who bring Buddhism to the West should understand this well. They should be able to go into the world of Western culture and see many values of the West as elements of Buddhadharma. Drug addiction, alcoholism, and sexual misconduct are ruining the lives of many young people, but we can look deeply and see into their true nature, we can transform them into Buddhadharma. When we look directly into the suffering, we will find answers. One philosopher said that a true question already contains the answer in it. When a teacher gives you a good math problem, the answer is already there.

When we say, "What gave birth to the cosmos?" no answer is possible because we have not asked a true question. In it is the assumption that the cosmos was born of a single cause, and no phenomenon was ever born of a single cause. Everything comes from innumerable causes. In a flower, there are soil, clouds, compost, consciousness, rain, and sun. Because "Who gave birth to the cosmos?" is not a true question, the answer cannot be found in it. If the sufferings of people due to drug addiction, alcoholism, and sexual misconduct can be correctly formed into a question, the answers will be found in it. When there is a true question, Buddhadharma is already there. The art of posing a question is very important.

If those who teach Buddhism in the West keep in mind that all dharmas are Buddhadharma, they will not feel like a drop of oil in a glass of water. If Westerners bring into their society an exotic expression of Buddhism, thinking that this particular form of Buddhism is the only true Buddhism, the oil will never dissolve into the water. Buddhism will only succeed here if it is built from your own experiences and with your own cultural ingredients. If you practice in exactly the same way we practice in Vietnam, Tibet, Thailand, Burma, Sri Lanka, Japan, or Korea, the oil drops will always remain separate from the water. As Western Buddhists, please use the many elements of your own culture to weave the fabric of Buddhadharma.

Although this part of the sutra sounds like the previous sections, when we read it carefully we find many new elements. "All dharmas are Buddhadharma" is a short sentence, but it reveals the deepest teachings of the Buddha.

"Subhuti, a comparison can be made with the idea of a great human body."

Subhuti said, "What the Tathagata calls a great human body is, in fact, not a great human body."

"Subhuti, it is the same concerning bodhisattvas. If a bodhisattva thinks that she has to liberate all living beings, then she is not yet a bodhisattva. Why? Subhuti, there is no independently existing object of mind called bodhisattva. Therefore,

the Buddha has said that all dharmas are without a self, a person, a living being, or a life span. Subhuti, if a bodhisattva thinks, 'I have to create a serene and beautiful Buddha field,' that person is not yet a bodhisattva. Why? What the Tathagata calls a serene and beautiful Buddha field is not in fact a serene and beautiful Buddha field. And that is why it is called a serene and beautiful Buddha field. Subhuti, any bodhisattva who thoroughly understands the principle of non-self and non-dharma is called by the Tathagata an authentic bodhisattva."

The Buddha says that *all* objects of mind are concepts, even the object of mind called bodhisattva. When we use the language of the dialectics of prajñaparamita, we practice according to the principles of non-self and non-dharma. All schools of Buddhism talk about non-self. The Sarvastivadin school said it this way, "Even though the self does not exist, dharmas do exist." The existence of these objects of mind (dharmas) gives the impression that the self exists. Mahayana Buddhism opens a different door and proclaims that even what we call objects of mind or dharmas are of a selfless nature. The teaching of no-self is applied not only to humans and so-called living beings but also to other objects such as a table or a house. Self and dharma are just concepts. They are like a game. We should begin meditation practice by looking deeply into things and not letting the mind entrap us in games of words, reasoning, or speculation.

Not only is emptiness the nature of human beings and other so-called living beings, but it is also the nature of those things we call dharmas, things, or inanimate objects. A true bodhisattva is one who sees no demarcations between organic and non-organic, self and non-self, living beings and non-living beings, bodhisattvas and non-bodhisattvas.

PART FOUR

Mountains and Rivers Are Our Own Body

18
REALITY IS A STEADILY FLOWING STREAM

"Subhuti, what do you think? Does the Tathagata have the human eye?"

Human eye is the eye we all have that can see flowers, the blue sky, and the white clouds. Does the Buddha, the Awakened One, have the ordinary human eye?

Subhuti replied, "Yes, World-Honored One, the Tathagata does have the human eye."
The Buddha asked, "Subhuti, what do you think? Does the Tathagata have the divine eye?"

"Divine eye" is the eye of gods that sees very near and very far and also sees in darkness and through obstacles.

Subhuti said, "Yes, World-Honored One, the Tathagata does have the divine eye."
"Subhuti, what do you think? Does the Tathagata have the eye of insight?"

The "eye of insight" is the eye that can see the true nature of non-self in living beings and the impermanent nature of all objects of mind. It is the eye of the *shravakas* and *pratyeka buddhas.*

Subhuti replied, "Yes, World-Honored One, the Tathagata does have the eye of insight."

"Subhuti, what do you think? Does the Tathagata have the eye of transcendent wisdom?"

The "eye of transcendent wisdom" is the eye of the bodhisattvas that can see the true nature of the emptiness of all objects of mind. It can see the nature of awakened mind and of the great vow. A bodhisattva with the eye of transcendent wisdom sees that he or she and all beings share the same nature of emptiness, and therefore his or her liberation is one with the liberation of all beings.

"Yes, World-Honored One, the Tathagata does have the eye of transcendent wisdom."

The Buddha asked, "Does the Tathagata have the Buddha eye?"

"Yes, World-Honored One, the Tathagata does have the Buddha eye."

"The Buddha eye" is the eye that can see clearly the past, the present, and the future, as well as the minds of all living beings in the past, the present, and the future.

These five questions and answers state that the Buddha has not only the Buddha eye, but also the eyes of the bodhisattvas, shravakas, gods, humans, and all other living beings. The fact that the Buddha has a human eye gives us a pleasant feeling. It makes us feel closer to the Buddha. It means that what the Buddha accomplished, we too have the ability to accomplish.

"Subhuti, what do you think? Does the Buddha see the sand in the Ganges as sand?"

Subhuti said, "World-Honored One, the Tathagata also calls it sand."

"Subhuti, if there were as many Ganges Rivers as the number of grains of sand of the Ganges and there was a Buddha land for each grain of sand in all those Ganges Rivers, would those Buddha lands be many?"

"Yes, World-Honored One, very many."

The Buddha said, "Subhuti, however many living beings there are in all these Buddha lands, though they each have a different mentality, the Tathagata understands them all. Why is that? Subhuti, what the Tathagata calls different mentalities are not in fact different mentalities. That is why they are called different mentalities."

Here, the Buddha begins to talk about the mind. This teaching is developed more extensively in the *Ratnakuta Sutra*, which made its appearance between the second and third centuries, particularly in the chapter named "The Manifestations of Consciousness." It also talks about the human eye, the divine eye, the eye of insight, the eye of transcendent wisdom, and the Buddha eye.

This section of the *Diamond Sutra* briefly explains the Buddha eye as the eye that can see into the minds of all living beings. The Buddha has a very profound insight into the mentality of all of these beings. The Buddha says that if there were as many Ganges rivers as the number of grains in the sand of the Ganges and if the number of worlds were as many as those grains of sand, he knows the mentalities of all living beings in all of these worlds. This means that the Buddha has a profound understanding of the mind. The mind here includes the mind understood by contemporary psychology as well as the roots and nature of all psychological phenomena, which are not conditioned by the birth and death of psychological phenomena.

Modern psychology only studies psychological phenomena at their surface level. In Buddhism, the study of the mind begins at the roots, so the Buddha sees both the phenomenal aspect of the different mentalities and also their true nature. The Tathagata understands all these different mentalities because what we call different mentalities are not, in fact, only different mentalities.

"Why? Subhuti, the past mind cannot be grasped, neither can the present mind or the future mind."

How can we have a true understanding of the mind if we keep going after different psychological phenomena trying to grasp them? This is why it is difficult for modern psychology to truly grasp the mind. In the practice of Buddhism, by means of direct experience, one is able to be in touch with the true mind. Psychological studies, research, theories, and comparisons of different mental phenomena cannot really grasp the mind, since the past mind cannot be grasped, neither can the present mind or the future mind. As soon as any mind arises, it immediately dissolves.

In this sutra, we learn how to deal with words and concepts. Words are used to name or describe concepts, but as soon as we see things as they are, we understand that both words and concepts are not the things themselves. Words and concepts are rigid and motionless, but reality is a steadily flowing stream. It is impossible to contain a living reality in a rigid framework. We should always bear this in mind when we are trying to describe anything. There is always some distance between our words or concepts and that which is being described.

There is a famous story of a monk in China who was on his way to visit Zen master Sung Tin in Long Dam. He stopped at the foot of the Zen master's mountain to spend the night in a small inn that was run by an old lady. The monk arrived holding a copy of the *Diamond Sutra,* and the old lady, who was well versed in the sutra, noticed it.

After a night's rest, the monk said, "Good morning, madam. May I have something to point my mind?" ("Pointing the mind" was the Chinese expression for breakfast.)

The old woman asked back, "What kind of mind do you want to point—the past mind, the present mind, or the future mind?"

The monk was unable to answer. Feeling ashamed of himself, he gave up his journey to meet the master and headed back home. He felt that if he could not even answer the question of an old innkeeper, how could he confront a true master.

If she had asked me the same question, I would have answered something like this: "I do not need past mind, present mind, or future mind. I am hungry and only want something to eat." I could have touched my empty stomach as I spoke. The idea that the past mind, present mind, and future mind cannot be grasped is an excellent idea, but it is still just an idea. We need to eat. This is a living reality. When you are hungry, you need your breakfast. Why should you be impressed by a talkative innkeeper?

19
GREEN
GREAT HAPPINESS

"What do you think, Subhuti? If someone were to fill the 3,000 chiliocosms with precious treasures as an act of generosity, would that person bring great happiness by his virtuous act?"

"Yes, very much, World-Honored One."

"Subhuti, if such happiness were conceived as an entity separate from everything else, the Tathagata would not have said it to be great, but because it is ungraspable, the Tathagata has said that the virtuous act of that person brought about great happiness."

This is to confirm the fact that it is possible to use words and concepts for true communication, as long as you are not caught by words and concepts. The way to avoid being caught by words and concepts is to see the nature of inter-being in everything.

20
THIRTY-TWO MARKS

"Subhuti, what do you think? Can the Tathagata be perceived by his perfectly formed body?"

"No, World-Honored One. What the Tathagata calls a perfectly formed body is not in fact a perfectly formed body. That is why it is called a perfectly formed body."

"What do you think, Subhuti? Can the Tathagata be perceived by his perfectly formed physiognomy?"

"No, World-Honored One. It is impossible to perceive the Tathagata by any perfectly formed physiognomy. Why? Because what the Tathagata calls perfectly formed physiognomy is not in fact perfectly formed physiognomy. That is why it is called perfectly formed physiognomy."

According to legend, the Buddha's perfect physiognomy consists of thirty-two special marks. But the Buddha and Subhuti both say that the Tathagata cannot be perceived by any bodily form. As with all other forms, bodily forms are given a name, but both names and forms are framed by ideas and concepts and therefore cannot contain the living, boundless reality. The same teaching concerning the use of words and concepts is found in the following sections.

21

INSIGHT-LIFE

"Subhuti, do not say that the Tathagata conceives the idea 'I will give a teaching.' Do not think that way. Why? If anyone says that the Tathagata has something to teach, that person slanders the Buddha because he does not understand what I say. Subhuti, giving a Dharma talk in fact means that no talk is given. This is truly a Dharma talk."

Then, Insight-Life Subhuti said to the Buddha, "World-Honored One, in the future, will there be living beings who will feel complete confidence when they hear these words?"

The Buddha said, "Subhuti, those living beings are neither living beings nor non-living beings. Why is that? Subhuti, what the Tathagata calls non-living beings are truly living beings."

When we can see the non-rose elements when looking at a rose, it is safe for us to use the word "rose." When we look at A and see that A is not A, we know that A is truly A. Then A is no longer a dangerous obstacle for us.

"Insight-life" is a title given to noble teachers who have attained transcendent understanding, such as Insight-Life Subhuti, Insight-Life Sariputra, and so on. If we keep in mind that reality cannot be framed by words, concepts, speech, or symbols, we can easily understand the Buddha's teachings in these sections of the sutra.

22

THE SUNFLOWER

Subhuti asked the Buddha, "World-Honored One, is the highest, most fulfilled, awakened mind that the Buddha attained the unattainable?"

The Buddha said, "That is right, Subhuti. Regarding the highest, most fulfilled, awakened mind, I have not attained anything. That is why it is called the highest, most fulfilled, awakened mind."

Here we come to the notion of non-attainment. If we think that the Buddha has achieved an independently existing attainment, this attainment cannot be called the highest, most fulfilled awakened mind. The moment the concept of highest, most fulfilled, awakened mind arises, the essence of highest, most fulfilled, awakened mind vanishes. This is why the Buddha says, "I have not attained anything."

Many years ago I wrote a poem about a sunflower. The sunflower here is prajñaparamita, transcendent understanding.

> Come dear, with your innocent eyes,
> look at the clear, blue ocean of Dharmakaya.
> Even if the world is shattered,
> your smile will never vanish.
> What did I gain yesterday?
> And what will I lose today?

Come dear,
I point my finger
at the world
filled with illusions.
Since the sunflower is already there
all the other flowers turn toward it to contemplate.

23
THE MOON IS JUST THE MOON

"Furthermore, Subhuti, that mind is everywhere equally. Because it is neither high nor low, it is called the highest, most fulfilled, awakened mind. The fruit of the highest, most fulfilled, awakened mind is realized through the practice of all wholesome actions in the spirit of non-self, non-person, non-living being, and non-life span. Subhuti, what are called wholesome actions are in fact not wholesome actions. That is why they are called wholesome actions."

Now we come to the nature of equality, *samata* in Sanskrit. Equality means "neither this nor that," neither liberating nor being liberated, neither I nor others, neither many nor few, neither high nor low. All objects of mind are equal and share the same nature of interbeing.

The "highest, most fulfilled, awakened mind" cannot exist independently of what is not the highest, most fulfilled, awakened mind. There is no teapot that exists independently of non-teapot elements. Clouds are oceans, oceans are clouds. Clouds do not exist independently of oceans, and vice versa. Because all objects of mind are neither high nor low, this is called "the highest, most fulfilled, awakened mind." In our thoughts, the moon may be full or new, bright or dim, present or not present, but the moon itself has none of those characteristics. The moon is just the moon. All objects of the mind are equal.

24
THE MOST VIRTUOUS ACT

"Subhuti, if someone were to fill the 3,000 chiliocosms with piles of the seven precious treasures as high as Mount Sumeru as an act of generosity, the happiness resulting from this is much less than that of another person who knows how to accept, practice, and explain the Vajracchedika Prajñaparamita Sutra to others. The happiness resulting from the virtue of a person who practices this sutra, even if it is only a gatha of four lines, cannot be described by using examples or mathematics."

This section repeats the idea expressed in section 19. Please refer to the commentaries offered in that section.

25
ORGANIC LOVE

"Subhuti, do not say that the Tathagata has the idea, 'I will bring living beings to the shore of liberation.' Do not think that way, Subhuti. Why? In truth there is not one single being for the Tathagata to bring to the other shore. If the Tathagata were to think there was, he would be caught in the idea of a self, a person, a living being, or a life span."

Reflection is necessary for insight. *The Diamond that Cuts through Illusion* has many repetitions such as the ones above, and the more we chant or read this sutra, the more deeply we penetrate its profound significance. If we read it only once, we may think we understand all of it, but this can be dangerous. Reading a sutra is like doing massage. Time and energy are necessary for success.

The Tathagata uses words and ideas in the same way as others—a flower is a flower, garbage is garbage, awakening is awakening, illusion is illusion, afflictions are afflictions—but the Tathagata does not get caught in names or ideas. We, on the other hand, are in the habit of looking at these things as fixed entities, and we may get caught up in our views. So the Tathagata chooses language that can help us look deeply and, gradually, become liberated.

Sometimes the Buddha speaks in a way that sounds as if there is a self. For example, he said, "Ananda, would you like to go up to Vulture Peak with me?" When he uses the word "Ananda," the idea of a person is used. In the sentence, "Would you like to go up to Vulture Peak with me?" the idea of a self is used. Although the Tathagata uses words and ideas like others, he is not caught by the words and ideas.

"Subhuti, what the Tathagata calls a self essentially has no self in the way that ordinary persons think there is a self. Subhuti, the Tathagata does not regard anyone as an ordinary person. That is why he can call them ordinary persons."

This is a very deep and beautiful sentence. A person is called an ordinary person but is, at the same time, a Buddha. By calling him or her an ordinary person, the Buddha is not being condescending. We say the word Buddha with respect and admiration. We never imagine that there could be an impure element in the body of a Buddha or a bodhisattva, because we do not want to be disrespectful. But the teachings of prajñaparamita say that the Buddha's five aggregates are also of an organic nature. The Buddha is made of non-Buddha elements. The pure is made of the impure.

In Buddhism, non-duality is the essential characteristic of love. In love, the person who loves and the person being loved are not two. Love has an organic characteristic. In light of interbeing, all problems of the world and of humankind should be solved according to the principles of organic love and non-dual understanding. These principles can be applied to solve the problems of the Middle East and the former Soviet Union. The suffering of one side is also the suffering of the other side. The mistakes of one side are also the mistakes of the other side. When one side is angry, the other side suffers, and vice versa. These principles can also be applied to solve environmental problems, such as the greenhouse effect and the depletion of the ozone layer. Rivers, oceans, forests, mountains, earth, and rocks are all our body. To protect the living environment is also to protect ourselves. This is the organic, non-dualistic nature of the Buddhist way of looking at conflicts, the environment, and love.

26
A BASKET FILLED WITH WORDS

"What do you think, Subhuti? Can someone meditate on the Tathagata by means of the thirty-two marks?"

Subhuti said, "Yes, World-Honored One. We should use the thirty-two marks to meditate on the Tathagata."

The Buddha said, "If you say that you can use the thirty-two marks to see the Tathagata, then the Cakravartin is also a Tathagata?"

Subhuti said, "World-Honored One, I understand your teaching. One should not use the thirty-two marks to meditate on the Tathagata."

In Buddhism there are many different methods of meditation. One is the meditation on the image of the Buddha. According to this method, one visualizes the Buddha with thirty-two serene and beautiful marks. Sometimes the name of the Buddha is called so that the image of the Buddha can appear more clearly in the mind of the practitioner, who then feels peaceful and calm. The monks were accustomed to this practice and did it whenever they wanted to see the image of the Tathagata. That is why Subhuti answers quickly, "Yes, World-Honored One. We should use the thirty-two marks to meditate on the Tathagata."

A Cakravartin is a king who keeps the wheel of righteousness turning throughout his reign. He, too, was said to have the thirty-two marks of a great person. In light of the *Diamond Sutra,* we should not identify the body of thirty-two marks with the Buddha. In fact, we should make just as great an effort to look for the Buddha where the thirty-two marks are absent—in stagnant water and in beggars who have leprosy. When we can see the Buddha in these kinds of places, we have a signless view of the Buddha. This is not to say that the meditation on the Buddha through the thirty-two marks is erroneous. To a new practitioner, this meditation can bring confidence, stability, and peace of mind.

> The precious lotus is blooming on the throne of
>   awakening.
> The Buddha's light reaches in the ten directions.

His understanding envelops the realm of all
    dharmas.
His love penetrates mountains and rivers.
On seeing the image of the Awakened One, I feel
    all my afflictions vanish.
I praise his boundless merit and vow to study and
    practice in order to attain
    the fruit of awakening.

While going through difficult moments in life, if we contemplate the Buddha with the thirty-two marks, we feel fresh and relaxed. The *Diamond Sutra* does not tell us not to do that. It just teaches us to look more deeply and to also meditate on the Buddha outside of the thirty-two marks. The Buddha will suffocate if we grasp him too firmly. One Zen master stopped using the word "Buddha" because people overused the word so. He told his community, "From now on, every time I use the word 'Buddha,' I will go to the river and wash my mouth out three times." His statement is completely in accord with the dialectics of prajñaparamita, but when people heard his words, they thought he was being disrespectful. Only one honored guest in the community understood. He stood up and said, "Venerable sir, I deeply appreciate your words. Every time I hear you say the word 'Buddha,' I will have to go to the river and wash out my ears three times." How wonderful! Both men were free of empty words. Those of us who use Buddhist terms without conveying the teaching of the Buddha should wash out our mouths and ears. We must be cautious. The Vietnamese musician Pham Duy wrote these words in his song *Man Is Not Our Enemy:*

Our enemy wears the colors of an ideology.
Our enemy wears the label of liberty.
Our enemy has a huge appearance.
Our enemy carries a big basket filled with words.

Then the World-Honored One spoke this verse:

"Someone who looks for me in form
or seeks me in sound
is on a mistaken path
and cannot see the Tathagata."

When we first learn to meditate, we may visualize the Buddha with his thirty-two special marks. We may even see the Buddha in our dreams. But once our wounds are healed, we should leave those images and see the Buddha in birth, sickness, old age, and death. Nirvana is made of the same substance as attachment, and awakening of the same substance as ignorance. We should be able to sow the seeds of awakening right here on Earth and not just in empty space. The beautiful lotus grows out of the mud. Without afflictions and suffering, we cannot make a Buddha.

This section of the sutra has taught us not to be bound by the idea of the thirty-two marks. We may come to think that the thirty-two marks are of no value, but, in truth, the practice of mindfulness always gives birth to beautiful marks. The fruits of practice—serenity, peace, and happiness—are truly there, but they cannot be seen in collections of views. They reveal themselves only in the wondrous reality.

27
NOT CUT OFF FROM LIFE

"Subhuti, if you think that the Tathagata realizes the highest, most fulfilled, awakened mind and does not need to have all the marks, you are wrong. Subhuti, do not think in that way. Do not think that when one gives rise to the highest, most fulfilled, awakened mind, one needs to see all objects of mind as nonexistent, cut off from life. Please do not think in that way. One who gives rise to the highest, most fulfilled, awakened mind does not contend that all objects of mind are nonexistent and cut off from life."

"Nonexistent" and "cut off from life" are also attachments. When we look at a table, a flower, or the highest, most fulfilled, awakened mind, if we see that they exist independently of other objects of mind, we are caught in the view of permanence. On the other hand, if we think that everything is nonexistent, we are caught in the view of annihilation. The middle way taught by the Buddha is a way free of these two views. Liberation is not to cut ourselves off from life or to try to reach nonbeing.

28
VIRTUE AND HAPPINESS

"Subhuti, if a bodhisattva were to fill the 3,000 chiliocosms with the seven precious treasures as many as the number of sand grains in the Ganges as an act of generosity, the happiness brought about by his or her virtue is less than that brought about by someone who has understood and wholeheartedly accepted the truth that all dharmas are of selfless nature and is able to live and bear fully this truth. Why is that, Subhuti? Be-

cause a bodhisattva does not need to build up virtue and hap-piness."

Subhuti asked the Buddha, "What do you mean, World-Honored One, when you say that a bodhisattva does not need to build up virtue and happiness?"

"Subhuti, a bodhisattva gives rise to virtue and happiness but is not caught in the idea of virtue and happiness. That is why the Tathagata has said that a bodhisattva does not need to build up virtue and happiness."

Whatever a bodhisattva thinks, says, and does can give rise to limitless virtue and happiness, but he or she is not caught in this. This is why the Buddha says that the bodhisattvas do not need to accumulate virtue and happiness. When we volunteer to wash the dishes, if we think that our work will bring us some happiness or merit in the future, we are not true bodhisattvas. We only need to live joyfully in each moment while we wash them. After they are washed, we don't need to tell everyone that we have just finished washing their dishes. If we do that, our work will have been a waste of time. Washing the dishes just to wash the dishes, on the other hand, brings us inestimable virtue and happiness.

We all know people who cannot bear great suffering, but we do not realize that to fully enjoy great happiness also requires great strength and endurance. The Sanskrit word for endurance is *kshanti*. It is one of the six paramitas. Only those who can bear great truth and great happiness are called mahasattvas. That is why in this section of the sutra we see the phrase: "[someone] who is able to live and bear fully this truth."

29

NEITHER COMING NOR GOING

"Subhuti, if someone says that the World-Honored One comes, goes, sits, and lies down, that person has not understood what I have said. Why? The meaning of Tathagata is 'does not come from anywhere and does not go anywhere.' That is why he is called a Tathagata."

Sometimes the Tathagata is defined as coming from suchness and going to suchness. This is meant to show us the nature of no coming and no going of all things. The ideas of coming and going cannot be applied to suchness. Suchness is suchness. How can suchness come and go?

So far the Buddha has talked about equality, non-duality, attachment to the view of permanence, and attachment to the view of annihilation. Now he tells us that reality is neither coming nor going. This truth does not apply only to the Tathagata. It applies also to all dharmas, all objects of mind.

30

THE INDESCRIBABLE NATURE OF ALL THINGS

"Subhuti, if a daughter or son of a good family were to grind the 3,000 chiliocosms to particles of dust, do you think there would be many particles?"

Subhuti replied, "World-Honored One, there would be many indeed. Why? If particles of dust had a real self-existence, the Buddha would not have called them particles of dust. What the Buddha calls particles of dust are not, in essence, particles of dust. That is why they can be called particles of dust. World-Honored One, what the Tathagata calls the 3,000 chiliocosms are not chiliocosms. That is why they are called chiliocosms.

Why? If chiliocosms are real, they are a compound of particles under the conditions of being assembled into an object. That which the Tathagata calls a compound is not essentially a compound. That is why it is called a compound."

"Subhuti, what is called a compound is just a conventional way of speaking. It has no real basis. Only ordinary people are caught up in conventional terms."

This passage is very important. At the time of the Buddha, it was thought that matter was formed by the coming together of atoms. Most people still think that way. Under proper conditions, atoms come together to form a table or a teapot. When we perceive a table or a teapot, we have an image in our mind of atoms coming together. That image is called a compound. Compound and atom thus become two opposite concepts. Only by seeing that atoms and compounds are not in themselves really atoms and compounds can we be freed from our erroneous concepts. If we think that anything is really a self-existent composite, we are caught by our attachment to that object of mind.

We cannot make any statement about the true nature of reality. Words and ideas can never convey reality. This passage of the sutra describes the indescribable nature of all things. If we base our understanding of reality on our concepts of particles, atoms, or composites we are stuck. We must go beyond all concepts if we want to be in touch with the true nature of things.

31
TORTOISE HAIR AND RABBIT'S HORNS

"Subhuti, if anyone says that the Buddha has spoken of a self view, a person view, a living-being view, or a life span view, has that person understood my meaning?"

"No, World-Honored One. Such a person has not understood the Tathagata. Why? What the Tathagata calls a self view, a person view, a living-being view, or a life span view are not in essence a self view, a person view, a living-being view, or a life span view. That is why they are called a self view, a person view, a living-being view, or a life span view."

"Subhuti, someone who gives rise to the highest, most fulfilled, awakened mind should know that this is true of all dharmas, should see that all dharmas are like this, should have confidence in the understanding of all dharmas without any conceptions about dharmas. Subhuti, what is called a conception of dharmas, the Tathagata has said, is not a conception of dharmas. That is why it is called a conception of dharmas."

Those who have not penetrated deeply into the meaning of the *Diamond Sutra* may think that the ideas of a self, a person, a living being, and a life span are the enemies of understanding, suchness, and the Tathagata. Because of that, they may want to eliminate these four ideas from reality. In this section, the Buddha gives us an antidote to that kind of dualistic thinking. He says that all dharmas—including self, person, living being, life span, non-self, non-person, non-living being, and non-life span—are concepts. We should not let go of one set of concepts just to be caught by another. The idea of non-self is born from the idea of self, just as a rose needs non-rose elements in order to exist.

When we look deeply into the concept of self, we can see the concept of non-self. Tortoise hair and rabbit horns do not exist in reality, but the ideas of tortoise hair and rabbit horns do. They are born from the ideas of hair, horns, tortoises, and rabbits. It is possible to look deeply into the reality of the ideas of tortoise hair and rabbit horns to see the true nature of the world, the true nature of suchness, and the true nature of the Tathagata.

The Buddha teaches us not to discriminate against the concepts of self, person, living being, and life span. These concepts are as valuable as the concepts of emptiness, suchness, Tathagata, and the highest, most fulfilled, awakened mind. All concepts co-arise and are empty of a separate self. If the highest, most fulfilled, awakened mind is empty, then the ideas of self, person, living being, and life span are also empty. So why should we discriminate or be afraid of them? All concepts are dharmas, objects of mind, signs. The Buddha tells us that whenever there is a sign, there is deception. The sign of self, person, suchness, or Tathagata all are subject to deception.

In light of the teachings of interbeing and dependent co-origination, all dharmas depend on one another to be born and develop. Look deeply into one dharma, and you will see all dharmas. This is explained in the *Avatamsaka Sutra*. Please keep in mind that to discriminate against the concepts of self, person, living being, and life span is to go after the opposite concepts. Once we understand that a concept is just a concept, we can go beyond that concept and be free of the dharma that concept represents. Then we can begin to have a direct experience of the wondrous reality that is beyond concepts.

32
TEACHING THE DHARMA

"Subhuti, if someone were to offer an immeasurable quantity of the seven treasures to fill the worlds as infinite as space as an act of generosity, the happiness resulting from that virtuous act would not equal the happiness resulting from a son or daughter of a good family who gives rise to the awakened mind and reads, recites, accepts, and puts into practice this sutra, and explains it to others, even if only a gatha of four lines. In what spirit is this explanation given? Without being caught up in signs, just according to things as they are, without agitation. Why is this?"

The Buddha is telling us how to teach this sutra to others. He says that we should explain it according to the way things are, without encouraging the listeners to be caught up in signs. He adds that we should stay calm, not agitated, while we teach.

If we observe someone who is sharing the sutra, we can usually tell whether he or she is doing it in the spirit of signlessness. By being observant, we can hear and feel whether the explanations have in them the idea that "I am the one who is teaching the sutra, and you are the listeners." In this way, we can tell to what extent the instructor is still caught in the concepts of self, person, living being, and life span. If he or she is heavily caught by those four concepts, their insights about the *Diamond Sutra* cannot be authentic. The spirit of the transcendent understanding can only be revealed by someone who is free of signs.

To explain the *Diamond Sutra*, a teacher must be in touch with suchness, the nature of non-duality, the truth that cannot be described. Being in touch with suchness is like digging a well and reaching the point where the water forces its way up. Once we can drink directly from the well of understanding, we are no longer caught by the signs of a self, a person, a living being, or a life span. When we see that someone is free of those signs, even if it is not yet complete, we know his or her teaching is authentic. Even if such a teacher is criticized or accused of explaining the sutra incorrectly, he or she will remain happy and at peace, with no signs of anger or agitation.

The Buddha offers us this gatha to end the *Diamond Sutra:*

> *"All composed things are like a dream,*
> *a phantom, a drop of dew, a flash of lightning.*
> *That is how to meditate on them.*
> *That is how to observe them."*

Composed things are all objects of mind that are conditioned to arise, exist for awhile, and then disappear, according to the principle of dependent co-arising. Everything in life seems to follow this pattern, and, although things look real, they are actually more like the things a magician conjures up. We can see and hear them clearly, but they are not really what they appear to be. A bubble, *timira* in Sanskrit, is an image that we can use to describe appearances. Or if we rub our eyes vigorously and see many stars, we may think the stars are real, but they are not.

After reading this verse, we may think that the Buddha is saying that all dharmas are impermanent—like clouds, smoke, or a flash of lightning. The Buddha *is* saying, "All dharmas are impermanent," but he is not saying that they are not here. He only wants us to see the things in themselves. We may think that we have already grasped reality, but, in fact, we are only grasping its fleeting images. If we look deeply into things, we will be able to free ourselves from the illusion.

We can even use scientific research to prove, to some extent, some sentences in this sutra. A table that looks firm and real, for example, may be only space and electrons moving like a swarm of bees at close to the speed of light. Nuclear physicists have said that while going into the subatomic world, they find our common, daily perceptions funny. Regardless of that, a physicist lives his ordinary life as other people do. He drinks tea, and eats bread like the rest of us, even though he knows that his piece of bread is made up mostly of space and a very small number of particles of matter. The same is true of the Buddha. The Buddha knows that all things are like a dream, a phantom, a bubble, a flash of lightning, but he still lives his life normally. He still eats and drinks. The only difference is that the Buddha lives his life in the spirit of signlessness and non-attachment.

After they heard the Lord Buddha deliver this sutra, the Venerable Subhuti, the bhikshus and bhikshunis, laymen and laywomen, and gods and asuras, filled with joy and confidence, undertook to put these teachings into practice.

Reciting the *Diamond Sutra* is one of several methods to practice and observe it. At night, you can sit quietly and recite this sutra. Recitation is a way to water the seeds of understanding that lie deep in the soil of our mind. If these seeds are watered infrequently, they will dry up. But if they are watered often, they will sprout and develop. Occasionally, in totally unexpected moments, you will come to a bright and profound realization. Don't be put off by the repetitive conversations between the Buddha and Subhuti. There are sayings that we need to repeat for ourselves throughout our lives. There are songs that need to be sung often. The more we sing them, the more we are penetrated by their meaning.

It has been wonderful to study this sutra with a group of friends. I am sure you will discover new things in the sutra every time you study it. In our community, whenever we complete a sutra study or recitation session, we join our palms and chant this gatha together, to show our gratitude to the Three Jewels: the Buddha, the Dharma, and the Sangha. Let us do it now:

> Reciting the sutras, practicing the way of
>   awareness,
> gives rise to benefits without limit.
> We vow to share the fruits with all beings.
> We vow to offer tribute to parents, teachers,
> friends, and numerous beings,
> who give guidance and support along the path.

Parallax Press publishes books on engaged Buddhism and the practice of mindfulness by Thich Nhat Hanh and other authors. For a free copy of our catalog, please visit our online bookstore or contact:

Parallax Press
P.O. Box 7355
Berkeley, CA 94707
www.parallax.org
Tel: (800) 863-5290

Monastics and laypeople practice the art of mindful living in the tradition of Thich Nhat Hanh at retreat communities in France and the United States. Individuals, couples, and families are invited to join these communities for a Day of Mindfulness and longer practice periods. For information, please visit www.plumvillage.org or contact:

Plum Village
13 Martineau
33580 Dieulivol, France
info@plumvillage.org

Green Mountain Dharma Center
P.O. Box 182
Hartland Four Corners, VT 05049
mfmaster@vermontel.net
Tel: (802) 436-1103

Deer Park Monastery
2499 Melru Lane
Escondido, CA 92026
deerpark@plumvillage.org
Tel: (760) 291-1003